BRINGING YOUR CHURCH BACK TO

BEYOND SURVIVAL MENTALITY

DANIEL BUTTRY

Judson Press ® V

BRINGING YOUR CHURCH BACK TO LIFE: BEYOND SURVIVAL MENTALITY
Copyright © 1988
Judson Press, Valley Forge, PA 19482-0851

Unless otherwise indicated, Bible quotations in this volume are from the Revised Standard Version of the Bible, copyrighted 1946, 1952 ©, 1971, 1973 by the Division of Christian Education of the National Council of the Churches of Christ in the U.S.A., and used by permission.

Other quotations of the Bible are from
The Holy Bible, King James Version.
HOLY BIBLE New International Version, copyright © 1978, New York International Bible Society. Used by permission.
Good News Bible, The Bible in Today's English Version. Copyright © American Bible Society, 1976. Used by permission.

LIBRARY OF CONGRESS
Library of Congress Cataloging-in-Publication Data

Buttry, Daniel L.
    Bringing your church back to life: beyond survival mentality / by
Daniel L. Buttry.
        p. cm.
    ISBN 0-8170-1143-9
    1. Church renewal. I. Title.
BV600.2.B84 1988
262'.0017—dc19   88-15897

Printed in the U.S.A.

95 96 97 98 99 00 01 02   11 10 9 8 7 6 5 4

To Lucas W. Buttry,
my father and a good pastor, who
died one month before I entered the pastorate
at Dorchester Temple.

"And he took up the mantle of
Elijah that had fallen from him, and
went back and stood on the
bank of the Jordan"
(2 Kings 2:13).

Contents

Introduction

*E*vangelism" and "Church Growth" were big words in the seventies and eighties. Always the sole coin of evangelicals, the words are now used widely in mainline churches also.

The word for the nineties is "Renewal." It is the underlying concern of mainline churches everywhere. Lack of vitality, dwindling congregations, and dwindling budgets all forecast the slow death of once vital and growing denominations and churches.

The fact that renewal must come about is seldom debated, but how it is to come about, of course, is a matter of some conjecture. A lot of church people believe that it is possible to be renewed simply through the right techniques. Based on the best sociological analysis and understanding of human behavior, a church needs only to write a mission statement, develop sound objectives, formulate correct strategies; and a renewed church is guaranteed!

Daniel Buttry, however, does not work very much at that end of renewal. In this excellent volume he does develop carefully (and scripturally) the basic motif of *Vision*—in fact, *God's* vision for your church. Constantly calling us back to the fact that the *misseo Dei* is our task, he says we have to discover that mission by first exegeting Scripture and only then examining our community.

Above all, Buttry unabashedly calls us to live by and

through the Holy Spirit. Charismatic in the finest and truest sense of the term, he reminds us that the vision can only be truly clear through the Spirit and that the vision will only become reality through the power of that same Spirit.

All of Buttry's teaching has the clear ring of truth and reality because it has been hammered out on the anvil of experience in Dorchester, a neighborhood of Boston.

Dorchester Temple Baptist Church found unusual renewal. But the measure of that renewal did not stop with how many were won to Christ or how many attended morning worship. Renewal, for Buttry, is measured in terms of incarnation. Are people more Christ-like in their personal piety and more loving in their koinonia? Do they have a closer walk with God, which issues in a passion to lead others to that faith and that life?

A renewed church is a corporate group (and body) to which it is fun to belong. Its worship is contagious. But it cannot look at the world with dry eyes because the Christ who called the church into being is terribly concerned that racism, sexism, ageism—injustice of any kind—be dealt with. The renewed church is concerned that its parish know the Good News in practical ways. So Dorchester Temple became a strong leader in the demand for low-cost housing!

Buttry's portfolio in American Baptist Churches' National Ministries is Peace. He works passionately toward that goal for society. At the same time he is a most committed evangelist.

His life, ministry, and this book reflect that marvelous holism.

Emmett V. Johnson
Director of Evangelism
American Baptist Churches in the U.S.A.

Preface

*A*s a young seminary graduate entering into my first pastorate, I had a lot of ideas, zeal, and very little experience. That I should have participated in the renewal of a church is a testimony to the grace of God. My own shortcomings and limitations both in gifts and in spiritual maturity became evident to me and to others in the congregation. Yet God used me and my brothers and sisters at Dorchester Temple in Boston, Massachusetts, to recreate a dynamic expression of the body of Christ out of the decay and despair that had set in during years of decline. I am grateful to have had a part in this renewal and to have shared so intimately with the members of Dorchester Temple.

My thanks must go first to my wife, Sharon. She has been my companion on this journey, through the days of tears and the days of joy. She met my frustrations with comfort, my discouragement with challenge, and my pride with loving honesty. By her own pain she opened me to parts of myself that became vital channels for God's grace to flow through my ministry. We have brought more wholeness to each other. Without her I would have quit before experiencing the truths contained in these pages.

The members of Dorchester Temple have my eternal gratitude. They gave to me even as I gave to them. They accepted me as I was, which was delightfully freeing for me as pastor. I have been blessed by the courage of the older members to press on to the challenges of renewal when so many others have chosen the security of survivalism. My contemporaries brought their zeal and freshness along with a willingness to build a community of faith with those already there. I thank the children of the church who brought life to us all, even with their noise and disruption. They often ushered in the presence of Christ with their unveiled honesty and acceptance of people for who they were.

As I neared completion of this book, it became time for me to leave the pastorate of Dorchester Temple. A person with a different constellation of gifts was needed to lead them further in their journey into God's fullness, whereas God's call was moving me into different channels. One sign that it was God's time for me to move was that the church was strong and could minister creatively apart from my direct involvement. The vision had become their own.

I owe a debt to many people who have helped shape my ideas in settings from seminary to denominational offices, from pastor's study to retreat center, from convention halls to kitchens. John Perkins, founder of Voice of Calvary in Mississippi, stimulated my thinking on vision and the work of vision bearing. I thank Rev. John Douhan for his critical interaction, which added a key chapter to my earlier conception of the book. Many of my co-laborers in pastoral ministry have enriched the pool of experience and knowledge from which I draw, sometimes entrusting their own wounds and sorrows to me.

I thank the members of the Personal and Public Witness Unit of National Ministries, American Baptist Churches in the U.S.A., especially Dr. Emmett V. Johnson, our unit manager. They have encouraged me to finish this book, which almost died just short of birth when I left Dorchester Temple. Their input and insight has strengthened the final product. I am glad to be a part of a team of people committed to a vision of holistic mission through a renewed church.

Finally, I am grateful for the work of the many people who moved the book from my scribbled drafts to final product. I am deeply appreciative to Joanne Powers, Kristy Pullen, Laura Alden, Pamela Roth, Nancy Copenhaver, Gloria Coursey, Tami Laws, Heidi Levengood, and Sandy Ruud. Producing a book takes a great deal of coordinated and skilled effort, and I thank all who had a hand in this particular endeavor.

Prologue: A Vision

*I*n 1976 Dorchester Temple Baptist Church in Boston had a big celebration for their ninetieth anniversary because, according to one member, they didn't think they would make it to their hundredth. Ninety years of Christian community and witness as a local church is worth celebrating, but the underlying fear that the church wouldn't survive to its centennial revealed a common spiritual disease: survival mentality.

The members of Dorchester Temple had ample reason to worry. In the 1950s there were five white American Baptist churches in Dorchester. By 1980 the number was down to two. In the thirties, Dorchester Temple's membership was over a thousand, with the Sunday school having almost a thousand members as well. People used to come early so they could get a good seat for the worship service, and Easter saw standing-room-only crowds. But by the late seventies the membership had plunged to under 150, and the average attendance at worship was 80. The church seemed to be sliding down a greased slope, and the only reason it still seemed so strong was that it had always been the largest of the Baptist churches in Dorchester.

Dorchester Temple was not unique by any means. Most white, mainline, urban churches are in a serious state of decline. Hundreds of churches have closed, or congregations have sold their facilities to newer ethnic congregations, and now some suburban churches are beginning to notice the same patterns in their church life. These suburban churches have reached a similar point many urban churches reached twenty years ago, cause for the warning lights to go on.

Whatever the reasons for the decline, when people begin to realize what is happening, they shift their mental gears and begin to develop survivalist thinking. As the decline accelerates, survival mentality becomes the shared psychology of the congregation. Fewer people are involved in the life of the church. The building looks shabbier. The programs shrink, and an atmosphere of despair lingers over the people of God. The church is dying. It may hang on for a long time due to the stubbornness and determination of the faithful saints, but the church is dying nevertheless. Is there any hope, any good news for the churches stricken with survival mentality? The prophet Ezekiel had a strange and marvelous vision that speaks hope to these dying churches:

> The hand of the LORD was upon me, and he brought me out by the Spirit of the LORD, and set me down in the midst of the valley; it was full of bones. And he led me round among them; and behold, there were very many upon valley; and lo, they were very dry. And he said to me, "Son of man, can these bones live?" And I answered, "O LORD GOD, thou knowest." Again he said to me, "Prophesy to these bones, and say to them, O dry bones, hear the word of the LORD. Thus says the LORD GOD to these bones: Behold, I will cause breath to enter you, and you shall live. And I will lay sinews upon you, and will cause flesh to come upon you, and cover you with skin, and put breath in you, and you shall live; and you shall know that I am the LORD."
>
> So I prophesied as I was commanded; and as I prophesied, there was a noise, and behold, a rattling; and the bones came together, bone to its bone. And as I looked, there were sinews on them, and flesh had come upon them, and skin had covered them; but there was no breath in them. Then he said to me, "Prophesy to the breath, prophesy, son of man, and say to the breath, Thus says the LORD GOD: Come from the four winds, O breath, and breathe upon these slain, that they may

live." So I prophesied as he commanded me, and the breath came into them, and they lived, and stood upon their feet, an exceedingly great host.

Then he said unto me, "Son of man, these bones are the whole house of Israel. Behold, they say, 'Our bones are dried up, and our hope is lost; we are clean cut off.' Therefore prophesy, and say to them, Thus says the LORD GOD: Behold, I will open your graves and raise you from your graves, O my people; and I will bring you home into the land of Israel. And you shall know that I am the LORD, when I open your graves, and raise you from your graves, O my people. And I will put my Spirit within you, and you shall live, and I will place you in your own land; then you shall know that I, the LORD, have spoken, and I have done it, says the LORD" (Ezekiel 37:1-14).

Many of our churches are as dry as the valley of bones Ezekiel saw, and God alone knows if they will ever live again. But, as the prophet prophesied, God's Spirit moved across the bones. The scattered pieces were joined together. The skeletons were fleshed out, and the living breath of God infused them with dynamic energy. These dead bones became a mighty army.

Ezekiel was addressing the despairing people of Israel who had seen their nation ravaged by Babylon, the holy city burned, the temple of God utterly destroyed. But God is in the resurrection business, and the Spirit will raise up these despairing, broken, exiled people and restore them to the place of promise. Our God is "the same yesterday and today and for ever" (Hebrew 13:8). The God who spoke to the dry bones of Israel speaks to the dry bones in Dorchester and every other despairing church. Survival mentality is a deadly disease, but it can be healed.

This book is being written to testify to God's healing work and to be a vehicle of encouragement and guidance for others to appropriate the gracious renewal of God. The first step is to understand the disease adequately. Therefore, the symptoms and workings of survival mentality will be set forth, including a ray of hope in the remnant people. Then the vision that inspires the new life will be outlined in Chapters 3 to 5. The key person is the vision bearer, the one who like Ezekiel prophesied to the bones. This role of vision bearer, a gift of ministry not often lifted up for analysis, will be explored in Chapters 6 and 7. Finally,. the barriers to renewal, both practical and spiritual, will be addressed. Certainly this study can't be exhaustive, but if it sparks a fresh vision, then it will have succeeded.

Survival Mentality

Survival mentality is a spiritual disease, a congregational cancer that is life threatening to the body of Christ in the form of a local church. In advanced cases the condition is clear and the symptoms stark. But in the early stages the symptoms can be ignored because the health and vitality of earlier years mask the gradual decline of church life. The problem cannot be avoided indefinitely, however.

Just as a human being wastes away and other people begin to notice the loss of weight and the gauntness of feature, the people within a declining church begin to become conscious of the decay. A cycle of hopelessness begins to take hold. Steps are taken to ease the pain by avoiding the root issues or applying superficial and sometimes counterproductive solutions. The result is that the decline just gets worse, and the despair gets deeper. To combat the disease we must study it fully.

The Symptoms
A. Goal of Survival

The first symptom is revealed in church goals. The churches that are in serious condition will state their goal as being to keep the doors open. It is as simple and blunt as that: we don't want to see God's business fold up; we just want to survive. "Don't close the doors" is hardly a soul-stirring slogan, yet that is precisely the vision at the core of survivalist thinking. Attracting new members is like trying to sign people up for a cruise with the premise "We don't want to sink." Who wants to travel on a sinking ship? Who wants to join a church whose inspiration comes from just keeping the doors open?

This goal can have a variety of subtler expressions. The concern may be explicitly stated for getting new people into the church or reaching the youth (of whom there are hardly any in the congregation). Such statements have hidden premises—that new people aren't coming, that the next generation is absent. These concerns are seldom analyzed to uncover the root issues. Nobody asks why the younger generation finds the church uninteresting. To probe into the issue is too threatening, so the desires of the church are phrased in safe-sounding ways. After all, what church doesn't want to bring in new members? What church doesn't want to reach the youth? But instead of these concerns springing from a fervor for mission, they cloak a fear of decline and eventual doom. The question of basic survival lurks in the background, seldom acknowledged, but always felt.

B. Memory as the Glue

So what holds a church together for so long? Churches are notoriously stubborn for hanging on through decades of decline, turmoil, schisms, and pastoral failures. A tenacious core holds on to the church, like a bulldog refusing to let go. I knew a congregation of fourteen people that staggered on with minimal pastoral leadership and a massive building. How could they do it?

There is a powerful glue that holds together the people in survivalist churches—memory. The glorious past of the church holds the loyalty of people whose lives were formed and transformed during that era. In Dorchester Temple, people recalled the grand services when the sanctuary was at standing-room capacity. They remembered the talent shows and the bowling leagues. They remembered the hurricane of '38 that sent the uprooted tree crashing through the largest stained glass window. They remembered the men working with saws to cut up the tree before the wedding scheduled for that Saturday. They remembered the Sunday school classes of fifty or even one hundred members, groups not only for religious instruction but also for friendship and fellowship. The family histories are especially powerful. They were married at this altar; their children were baptized here and often married here. The memorials to sons lost in war are still close, such as the cross in front of the baptistry, the organ chimes. These memories are a mighty bond, for to let the church die is to let one's history die. Even for those who have moved away there is great comfort in knowing the old church is still there, for that's where one's past lies. It is still alive, so their history is a living history.

Those who remain are the caretakers of the past, the curators of a museum. They keep in touch with former members, letting them know the old church still has its doors open. The past is talked about with fondness, the smiles light up, the good times can almost be felt. But the future is a far different matter. It is best not talked about at all. Who talks honestly with a dying relative about his or her approaching death? Many members of the family and friends will enter an unspoken but mutually accepted conspiracy of ignoring the central fact of this present moment, and the same is true in survivalist churches. Small talk is made because everyone is too frightened to contemplate what the future holds. The past is our glue, but the future threatens to dissolve that glue. Therefore, it is best avoided in the minds of the loyal survivalists.

C. Fear of Change

A survivalist church has very little capital to invest in any unguaranteed venture. It has a short supply of financial capital. The Sunday collections seldom meet the budgeted needs, and the result in many churches is that endowments are spent to balance the annual financial statement. But financial capital is not the only resource in scarce supply. The human capital is also very limited. Usually churches stricken with survival mentality have memberships that are both shrinking and aging. The leadership pool is at one and the same time getting smaller and older. There are fewer talented people in the congregation, fewer spiritual gifts to be experienced. Aging contributes to the problem, for as one old, committed deacon put it, "The spirit is willing but the flesh is weak." Leaders who love the Lord and love the church experience great frustration when they see the problems increasing, but their own energy to invest in problem solving is decreasing.

Because of the shortage of human and financial capital, there is a powerful conservative force against any suggestion of change. To make a change is to take a risk. Nobody knows if the risk will lead to a profitable experience or a disaster. In churches there is a strong tendency to hold on to what the church already has. In a state of decline, a poverty of resources leads to conservation of these resources for the sake of survival. To put them at risk is to risk one's own survival, so such a risk is only taken if there is no other option.

Of course, there are many reasons why people are hesitant to make changes: comfort, familiarity, laziness, apathy. Maybe the people's needs are being met, so why tamper with something that is working okay? Then there are the people who are hesitant because they don't see clearly what the costs or promises of a proposed change are. They ask questions, delay for the sake of further study, then only decide when the picture has become much clearer. These legitimate, and even the nonlegitimate, conservative factors signal survival mentality. The key ingredient is fear. Change is resisted not because people's needs are being met, though they may be to a large extent. Change is resisted not because people are comfortable with their familiar patterns and styles, though most likely they are. Change is resisted because of fear. The threat of failure looms extra large because there is so little left to lose. If any money is foolishly spent, if any big giver is offended, if any family leaves the church, it is felt as another nail driven into the coffin of a dying church which nobody wants to let die.

Fear of change is blind, however. Change is always taking place. Neighborhoods change, families change, people grow older. Social values shift, new styles develop. The issues of one generation become irrelevant or are passed to the next. The church that fears change doesn't stay in the same place! It goes backwards, it retreats. It draws into a self-protective inwardness where patterns and traditions are kept stable and predictable in contrast to the shifting world outside. The church becomes self-serving out of fear. All thought of mission efforts to the community evaporate, for mission is a risky business. Because there is so much to lose and they fear putting their limited capital at risk, the survivalist church becomes a spiritual tortoise, pulled into its shell, safe and secure, but going nowhere.

D. Control-oriented Leaders

Because so much is at stake, including the church's very survival, those who are in positions of power often become very control-oriented. They hold tightly onto the decision-making process, unwilling to trust anyone who hasn't shared their struggle against decline.

Often power games are indulged in by the leadership, which is nothing unusual for churches. Power games and striving to control are very appealing tactics to churches in survival mentality.

I am the type of person who likes to be in charge in a crisis. When my wife and I get lost driving in the car, I work best when I am at the wheel and looking at the map, even if it was my poor choices that got us lost in the first place. I trust myself more than anyone else in such a situation. Many church leaders, deacons, trustees, and elders operate in the same fashion. The church is lost, and their poor choices have sometimes contributed to that lostness. But they are in the driver's seat. Nobody loves the church like they do, and they may be right. They have proven their love and faithfulness over the years of decline. While everyone else was jumping ship and moving away, they stayed on board and did all the hard work of keeping the ship afloat. Their sacrifices and dedication are unmatched and may prove to be an invaluable commodity in rebuilding the church.

But in survival mentality, such sacrifice and dedication can be used as justification to lock others out of the decision-making process. A clique, a family, or even an individual will dominate the centers of power. It's easy to gain control since all the resources are so limited. By one's financial giving or one's willingness to do the critical jobs, a person can become indispensable. Nobody dares cross this individual who might then become offended and leave. Fear then dictates the decision-making process, and it is easy for a person in the dominating position to manipulate church business as he or she desires. Sometimes pastors become the victims of their political games. They may labor with a profound Christian dedication and sense of mission, but the church is not operating in a healthy manner.

The control games effectively lock new people out of the decision-making process. Newcomers will never be able to match the dedication and sacrifice piled up over the years, so if there isn't a measure of trust to welcome them into positions of leadership, they will find no place to use their gifts. Locking newcomers out feels safe, for newcomers bring the possibility of change, which is unsettling to survivalist church members. The new generation thinks differently, has different styles, different concerns, and different interests. If they aren't related to the older members or if they are from a different ethnic or racial group, then the gap grows wider. The newcomers will change what the church is by their active involvement; it won't be so comfortable and familiar. So those in control have to try to hold on, for if the comfortable and familiar goes, what is left?

One church I know tried to open up the decision-making process by changing the bylaws so that new members could join the key boards more quickly. The small clique that was the main power in the church called all the members who had moved away but were still on the rolls. Because enough of these merely technical members came out for the business meeting to vote against the proposed changes, the clique was able to kill the new bylaws. But they killed more than a document. They killed the interest and enthusiasm of the newcomers who were willing to serve and take their share of responsibility for the life of the church. They killed the hopes of the pastor who was laboring for renewal. They killed an opportunity for their church to take a step out of survival mentality. All in the name of love for their dear old church.

E. Money-oriented Attitude

The final symptom is perhaps the easiest to spot. Survivalist churches are money-oriented. As the church declines, the financial base declines as well. Fewer people are present to give money, and as the congregation ages, more of the members begin living on fixed incomes. Though program budgets may shrink, the costs of maintaining an old building mount as the lack of proper maintenance turns small problems into major problems. The resulting convergence of these factors is that money issues become the focus of the desperate struggle to keep the doors open. If the bills aren't paid, the whole operation will be forced to shut down.

The money squeeze of survivalist churches has far-reaching consequences in the life of the congregation. It creates a severe leadership problem. Because of shrinking income, the church is able to offer only a minimal salary for a full-time pastor, or perhaps only a part-time position can be funded. Few clergy with much experience will be attracted to a pastoral opening with hardly enough salary for him or her to survive, especially if there is a family to support. The result is that such churches go to recent seminary graduates to fill their pulpits or to older pastors serving a few more years before retirement. The toughest churches to lead can't afford the best leaders to take on their challenges. The church can then get into a vicious cycle of quick-turnover pastorates. Pastors either retire if they are old or move on to a "better," more financially stable position if they are young.

A tight budget and the fear of taking risks means very few if any steps will be taken to reach out to the surrounding community in evangelistic or social witness. It takes money even to buy tracts and Bibles to pass out, and if there is no guaranteed return, many churches cannot bring themselves to risk the investment. Mission dollars may continue to trickle overseas, for to shut down all missions giving would be tantamount to giving up the faith, but the limited budget kills any new effort to reach out before it can even get a fair hearing.

The money problems work together with control issues in a mutually reinforcing way. The people who control the money will use their financial leverage to control other dimensions of church life. Big givers use their threats to cut back their pledges or to pull out of the church. The trustees (or whatever name they are called) become the board of final appeal. They exercise veto power over everything that goes on, for they control the purse strings.

Finally, stewardship becomes a wrestling match between bill-conscious trustees and guilt-ridden members. The financial campaign is characterized by pleas to help pay the bills and manipulative tactics to raise the guilt level high enough to pry loose a few more dollars. But such efforts are inevitably counterproductive. They create an image of the church as a beggar, and even people who give to beggars seldom like them. Visitors will be turned off when they hear these appeals, thinking, *Here is another church that is just after my money, and look how little it provides in return!* The members will tend to give below their potential because they, too, are affected by the beggar image. In their case the beggar is themselves, so their collective self-esteem is very low. If you don't love yourself, you won't spend much for yourself. Members may be able to give more than they do, but the subconscious distaste for what they have become limits the degree of financial sacrifice they will make. Deep down they know the church is not a good investment. They are not the cheerful givers the Lord loves but discouraged givers shelling out under guilt to keep an unpleasant future at bay for a little while longer.

The Patient

Patients in a hospital all have their own unique stories and physical constitutions, but that does not mean a doctor must begin from scratch in seeking to understand each one's particular affliction. There are common illnesses, symptoms, and treatments that doctors have learned through millions of case studies over the years, both in their own experience and in the pool of experience shared through schools, textbooks, and professional journals. Despite its unique characteristics, a case study can reveal more concretely the nature of a disease, its manner of development, and the best methods to be used in treatment.

The patient with survival mentality I knew most intimately was Dorchester Temple. This church's history will be examined as a case study to show concretely the nature of the disease and its treatment by God, the Master Physician.

Dorchester Temple was founded in 1886 as a missionary church of the Tremont Temple Baptist Church, a grand historic church in downtown Boston. Dorchester was a semirural area growing into a suburb of Boston. The church was initially founded around a Sunday school outreach, and in less than four years the membership was up to 100. In 1897 the church began a branch Bible school that quickly grew to 189 members and in 1900 became a church itself. Missionaries were sent from Dorchester Temple to Alaska, the Congo, China, and Burma. Young people from the church went into the pastoral ministry, and lay people were leaders in the denomination, the YMCA, and the political and business arenas. In 1928, while Dorchester became a more congested, middle-class suburb, the church reached a peak of 1,131 members with a Sunday school enrollment of 1,032.

After World War II new dynamics affecting religious life and urban society across the nation influenced Dorchester Temple.[1] Churches that had once been centers of all social life (Dorchester Temple had athletic teams, dramas, and entertainment programs) found themselves competing more and more with schools, community organizations, and even television for the free time of their members. With the increasing availability and affordability of automobiles, the American suburban dream was born. The nation's highway system was expanded, Federal Home Administration mortgages brought within reach new homes away from the crush of city life, and the suburbs sprang up around American cities. The children who went to Sunday school in Dorchester Temple during the twenties and thirties moved to Braintree, Weymouth, Randolph, and other southern suburbs of Boston. There they raised their families and often went to church.

Back in Dorchester new people were moving into the neighborhood. Irish Catholics had been moving into Dorchester from South Boston for a long time, and they became the overwhelming majority. The Baptists of Dorchester had more bigotry than evangelistic love for their Catholic neigh-

---

[1]See Raymond J. Bakke and Samuel K. Roberts, *The Expanded Mission of "Old First" Churches* (Valley Forge: Judson Press, 1986), pp. 27–30, for a description of these dynamics.

bors, so as members left for the suburbs, nobody was coming in to take their places.

Then in the late sixties and early seventies, a second population change occurred around Dorchester Temple. Blacks began moving in from Roxbury. With racial tension high, white members who had moved to the suburbs felt no compelling reasons to come back to a church in a neighborhood they viewed as unsafe. The people who remained were older members who were rapidly decreasing in number. A few new black members began joining, but some of the older white folks viewed their involvement not as a sign of hope, but as a sign of doom. The old Dorchester Temple was slipping away from them.

Various efforts were made to reverse these downward trends. One dynamic pastor spurred an increase in attendance and participation, but after he left the slide resumed. In the early seventies extensive conversations were held regarding the possibility of merger with two other Baptist churches who were also experiencing decline. The talks broke down, and each of the churches continued on its own downward way.

By 1978 the church was solidly stuck in survival mentality. The endowment was gone, the building was suffering from structural neglect, the congregational leadership was primarily seventy years old or more with very few people in sight to take their places. No outreach was going on toward the community other than an all-black youth group with black leadership. There was an atmosphere of despair and fatalism not far beneath the surface in spite of the determination, self-sacrifice, and piety of many of the members.

Other churches with survival mentality will have different stories with different emphases, but the themes will be much the same. The symptoms of survivalism are found in most of the cases I've encountered. The differences may reflect why some churches hang on for decades and others die quickly, why some turn around in dramatic fashion and others more gradually, and why ideas that work in one place fizzle miserably in another. Medical patients don't respond to treatments in the same way; what brings life to one causes an allergic reaction in another. However, enough similarities do exist to be able to identify the disease and to prescribe the treatment with the greatest likelihood of success. Whatever your patient's story is, then, consider carefully the symptoms and the treatment outlined in this case study.

The Prognosis

Churches that have developed survival mentality will die unless a major healing takes place. The disease is terminal. Sometimes its final phase is accelerated by pressures of splits, neighborhood changes, financial collapse, or fire. But even if it staggers on for twenty more years, its doom is sure.

All the symptoms of survival mentality build upon one another, creating a negative, downward spiral. Attempts to treat just the symptoms are bound to be misguided. They may postpone the death of the church, but they cannot give it a new life. Usually only superficial responses to the problem are taken: a new pastor is sought, an every-member canvass is undertaken, emergency aid is sought from the denomination. Each of these actions may be appropriate, but they do not get to the root issue. They do not expose the disease behind all the symptoms.

The root disease is a lack of vision. The basic vision that fuels the fires of renewal and growth has died out. The words are probably still there. Everyone knows the biblical passages and the cherished hymns, but the dynamic reality of Christ present in the church has been lost. Individuals may have deep and profound faith, but the group consciousness, the shared vision, the faith of the body of Christ has been swamped by a sea of despair. The meaning of the word "vision" in Proverbs 29:18 in the King James Version originally referred to the prophetic word: "Where *there is* no vision, the people perish." Although the contemporary understanding of the word "vision" refers to a clearly perceived goal, the meaning is still valid. Without a vision the church perishes. Survival mentality is at its root a disease of vision deficiency.

However, there is good news in spite of the diagnosis and prognosis. Though the disease of survival mentality is terminal, the Lord of the church, Jesus Christ, is a healer and even a raiser of the dead. Just as Jesus told the father of a sick child, "All things are possible to one who believes" (Mark 9:23, adapted), he comes to the dying churches and says, "All things are possible to the church that believes." That means anything can happen, even renewal and growth.

The response of the father to Jesus is an appropriate place to begin: "I believe; help my unbelief!" (Mark 9:24). Our churches are filled with doubt and fear. Yet the sparks of faith have not been fully extinguished. If we can lift our eyes to the Lord of the church and be renewed in faith, if we can catch a vision of who Christ is, what he can do, and what he calls us to, then the survivalist churches can leave their sickbeds of despair and take new, strong steps into the future. A new vision—a Christ-centered, Christ-inspired vision—is the only hope for the desperately ill congregation.

The members of Dorchester Temple can testify to the power of Christ to heal sick churches and raise up dying congregations. By 1986 Dorchester Temple had become a vibrant church. Attendance averaged 120 instead of 70, but over 90 percent of those active in the church had joined since 1978. The largest age groups were people in their twenties and thirties. The church had gone from having no nursery to having two and considering a third. Though the net numerical increase may not be stunning in church growth terms, the makeup of the congregation broke the rules for homogeneity: there were twelve different ethnic groups represented in the congregation, and people came from five major streams of Christian tradition—black Baptist, white Baptist, Charismatic/Pentecostal, high-church/liturgical,

and evangelical social activist traditions. The coming together of all these people created an exciting (and often
stressful) dynamic that gave birth to creativity in worship
and a lot of fun. The church was reaching out to the community with street evangelism, vacation Bible schools, social
ministries, and peace efforts. The church had left its sickbed
and was once again a growing (complete with growing
pains) body for Christ.

The Remnant

A church caught in survival mentality can look like Israel during the days of Isaiah. In Isaiah 1, the prophet describes the nation as a wounded, diseased body:

> The whole head is sick
>   and the whole heart faint.
> From the sole of the foot even to the head,
>   there is no soundness in it,
> but bruises and sores
>   and bleeding wounds;
> they are not pressed out, or bound up,
>   or softened with oil.
>   . . .
> If the LORD of hosts
>   had not left us with a few survivors,
> we would have been like Sodom,
>   and become like Gomorrah.
>   —Isaiah 1:5b-6,9

If there had not been a remnant of faithful ones left, a "few survivors," the nation would have been utterly lost.

Even in the gloomiest days God had a remnant of faithful people. Elijah was filled with self-righteous pity as he fled from Jezebel's wrath. He cried out to the Lord, "I, even I only, am left . . ." (1 Kings 19:10). The Lord corrected Elijah's shortsighted vision, "Yet I will leave seven thousand in Israel, all the knees that have not bowed to Baal, and every mouth that has not kissed him" (1 Kings 19:18). The Lord's people are there even when hidden by the decay and decline around them.

The faithful remnant becomes the seed for a new future. Isaiah's contemporary, Micah, proclaimed God's word of hope:

"I will surely gather all of you, O Jacob;
 I will surely bring together the remnant of Israel;
 I will bring them together like sheep in a pen,
  like a flock in its pasture,
  the place will throng with people."
                                    —Micah 2:12, NIV

Jeremiah announced God's deliverance out of disaster and the rebuilding of the nation through the remnant:

"Then I will gather the remnant of my flock out of all the countries where I have driven them, and I will bring them back to their fold, and they will be fruitful and multiply. I will set shepherds over them who will care for them, and they shall fear no more, nor be dismayed, neither shall any be missing, says the LORD" (Jeremiah 23:3-4).

Those who remain faithful, who hang on, "hoping against hope" as they wait for the Lord's restoration, will be the ones God uses to rebuild in the future. The faithful remnant is present in most churches struggling to survive.

God's Faithful People

Though many folks have left survivalist churches, moved to the suburbs, passed away or drifted away, there are those who stay and give of themselves year in and year out, even with little reward for their labors. One deacon poured his heart into the church, and as the winds of renewal began to blow, he felt out of place. He didn't belong anymore. But he stayed through the hard times, and he stayed through the times of transition. He left only when he knew the church wouldn't suffer from his departure. He had seen so many who had abandoned the church when it was being buffeted by neighborhood changes and flight of the members from the city. He stayed, and his grit and determination, along with others, enabled the torch to be passed to a new generation. This deacon will never win great acclaim, for his role was hidden to most human eyes, but he was one of the Lord's faithful remnant.

There are the people who accept the positions and responsibility in the church and shoulder their tasks with an attitude of servanthood. They resist the temptation to grasp and control. I know a couple who served in numerous capacities, but they were very clear that their service was a charge from God. They could have manipulated and dominated, but instead they gave of themselves with loving dedication. They, too, were a part of the remnant.

There are people who can see the challenges that need to be met if the church is to step into the future. One of the deacons approached me when I first came to Dorchester Temple and said, "We're going to have to develop some black leadership in this church." The leadership was almost exclusively white at the time, though at least a third of the congregation was black. If Dorchester Temple was going to move into the future, the multiracial nature of the congregation and the community necessitated a broadening of the leadership base. It would feel safer and easier to ignore such a concern and not put forth the effort to break down barriers of prejudice and distrust, but this deacon was courageous enough to think of the challenges to be met if the church was to have a long-range future.

Every person who came through our doors met two men who welcomed newcomers into the heart of the church. Instead of hanging around with only their long-standing friends, these men greeted visitors with a warmth that swelled up from deep within them. Every church claims to be friendly, but often they are friendly only to themselves. The church can become a close-knit mutual admiration society that makes everyone inside the circle feel great. Outsiders, however, feel they can never penetrate the circle, particularly if various fellowship groups or societies are closed. But these two men opened the relational door of the church so newcomers could enter the fellowship circle and begin to forge the bonds of new friendship.

The Central Issue

Undergirding the actions and attitude of these faithful ones is a genuine faith in the living Christ. Through all the ups and downs of the church's life, the remnant people have an abiding love for the Lord which is translated into faithfulness and perseverance. They may be discouraged. They may be frustrated. They may be at a loss as to what to do, but they really believe. They nourish within them the sparks of vision. They pray for revival, and they wait for it with deep longing. When the spirit moves, these will be the ones ready to move as well.

Roy and Muriel were a retired couple who had been in the church for decades. In earlier days Roy had played violin for the worship services, but now his fingers were too stiff to make sweet music. They were simple folks who could talk about their love for Christ and could pray with heartfelt passion. They gave freely of themselves to those in need around them, cared for the sick, and welcomed the stranger. Many hardships had come their way, including the loss of Roy's pension when his company went bankrupt, but their faith kept them full of love and joy that overflowed to people around them.

When the sparks of renewal began to burn, Roy and Muriel were excited. The joy and love deep within them resonated with the growing joy and love of the congregation. Their faith in Christ was such that they could see and affirm God's work even in forms with which they were unfamiliar. The result was that Roy and Muriel became key bridge people between the old and new. They helped provide leadership during the time of transition and could encourage the new life in the church and make significant caring relationships with new members. They became mom and dad to the whole congregation.

The contrast between those who stayed, like Roy and Muriel, and those who faded away during the renewal can, with a few exceptions, be focused on how their faith was expressed. When I went on pastoral visits and talked to folks, I experienced two dramatically different sorts of conversations. Besides all the sharing about family, work, and personal problems, some people could talk about what Christ meant to them and what he had done in their lives. Biblical knowledge or theological sophistication may or may not have been evidenced, but it was clear that Christ personally meant a great deal to them and was important in shaping their outlook and attitudes. The other folks would seldom if ever talk about God. They could talk extensively about the church, activities they had participated in, people they had known, how things had been accomplished; but when the conversation moved toward personalized talk about Jesus, they would shift the subject or be quiet.

While I cannot judge the faith of another, I could observe different responses to renewal that seemed to correlate clearly to the way people articulated the meaning of their church experience. It was similar to Jesus' parable about wineskins: "And no one puts new wine into old wineskins; if they do, the wine will burst the skins, and the wine is lost, and so are the skins; but new wine is for fresh skins" (Mark 2:22, adapted). The folks who could only talk about the activities they had been a part of and the people they had known were focused on the wineskins. The problem was that the wineskins had become brittle and cracked. The network of relationships was disintegrating as people died or moved away. Programs were folding from lack of interest or participation. If such long-term relationships and events were the central issue for their involvement in the church, then nothing would be left to sustain their commitment. Change was sweeping away the meaning of the church for them.

On the other hand, those who expressed their relationship with Christ as being at the heart of their church life were focused on the new wine. They could adapt to the changes of renewal and new people because the common bond was not any form of worship, shared memories, or social circle. The common bond was the living Christ whom they could share in ever richer and fuller ways. These folks were energized as the renewal spread; the others eventually found other churches to attend or dropped out altogether. Meanwhile, Roy, Muriel, and other like-minded remnant folks became the dependable core for the new Dorchester Temple.

Finding the Remnant

It may not be obvious at first which people in the church are those folks who will play pivotal roles in renewal. Some people in key positions will fall away. Many of the remnant people aren't even in leadership positions in survivalist churches. Perhaps they've been muscled out by those fearfully grasping for control. Often they are overlooked because they seem too simple for leadership. But in the proper setting, their strengths will become manifest. As they are drawn to a clear vision, they will be the ones to rally to the call with the toughness of a faith tried by long, hard times in the wilderness. People who have never been recognized as specially gifted may turn out to be surprising treasures. How are these people found?

First and foremost, they must be loved. The pastor who would shepherd a flock that is scattered and dismayed must show he or she loves the sheep. Nothing can replace the basic ministry of pastoral visitation and getting to know people on a one-to-one, heart-to-heart basis. This isn't such an awesome task in most survivalist churches because there aren't that many people to visit. The pastor must demonstrate and communicate unconditional love so that when steps toward a new future are taken, they are not put forth from an adversarial position. Without love, renewal won't happen. It cannot be a means to the end of building up a church. It must be an end in and of itself. As Paul says, "Let love be genuine . . ." (Romans 12:9). The people will know, and they will respond to a shepherd who loves them.

Bessie was a retired woman who cared for her ailing and confused husband. She had been the only person to vote against my call to the church, a fact which she confessed to me later (the vote had been reported to me as unanimous). I often visited her and helped her with issues regarding care for her husband. Our family had her and her husband over for Thanksgiving dinner. Soon she began to trust my pastoral care and commitment, and as she saw the renewal taking place in the church, she volunteered to use her gifts. Nobody had called on Bessie before, but when the church treasurer moved to Montana, she offered to fill this major position. She served ably as treasurer through our times of transition until her death a few years later. Through love Bessie had been given the inspiration and opportunity to use her gifts which nobody had known existed.

. Second, the people as a whole must be accepted as sufficient. God has given each congregation all it needs to take the next steps in following God's call. Nobody else is needed. No outside gifts are necessary. The temptation is to bemoan all that is missing. Nine months after I arrived at Dorchester Temple, our choir folded because the director, who was also the treasurer, custodian, and a deacon, moved away. Nobody was there to take his place. Some members even fell into the stereotypical pattern of asking my wife to direct the choir, she who had only sung in a choir for a few months! I told people that if God wanted us to have a choir, God would have to call a choir director. Nobody felt called, so that was the end of the choir. There were grumblings about how bad it was without a choir, but God was able to renew the church and move strongly ahead without one. Even years later we still had no regular choir. Renewal can and does begin with the people who are there, not those who aren't there. So a powerful message of acceptance needs to be expressed. The members need to hear that they are sufficient to do what God requires now. If God wants something done further down the line, a task that is currently beyond the abilities in the congregation, God will either provide a newcomer who can fit the bill or develop new gifts among the current members.

Third, people must be asked and challenged to share in shaping the future. The vision of the future is like a magnet, and the remnant will be drawn to that vision. It may take time to win their trust, but because of their deep abiding faith, they will be willing to step out once that trust is established. Two of our deacons, Roy and Harold, responded to the challenge of chairing our board during major times of transition. They both had the vision for the future, though they had long ties to the past. Under their leadership they moved the deacon board beyond conversations about how to take up the offering and keep the kids quiet during the worship service to the substantive issues about making a new way toward a new future. The interim pastor just prior to my coming to Dorchester Temple was a man of vision. He challenged one new black member to take on the youth group. Jackie had caught a vision for the future, too, and she accepted the challenge. Under her leadership the youth group and other outreach efforts to children became a significant component of the renewal process.

As the vision is lifted up, people will separate themselves like oil and vinegar. The remnant will rise to the top, and those who persist in survivalist thinking will tend to drift away. Unfortunately this process may not always be benign, and the conflict that can develop will be addressed in a later chapter. For the sake of renewal, though, the point is that a biblically based, Spirit-inspired vision will attract people. They will be sifted out of their traditional places and emerge as the foundation blocks for rebuilding the spiritual house of God.

The Vision of God

O nce one recognizes that God has a remnant in a church that is mired in survival mentality, the major challenge has to be faced: How does a church move from survival mentality to renewal? Often the question is asked as if the one who raised it expected to find a misplaced set of directions. Unfortunately churches do not come with a label saying "some assembly required" and an instruction sheet inside the box to assist the do-it-yourselfer. Renewal is more like human birth, or even rebirth. Jesus spoke to Nicodemus of the mystery of rebirth: "The wind blows where it wills, and you hear the sound of it, but you do not know whence it comes or whither it goes; so it is with everyone who is born of the Spirit" (John 3:8). There is mystery at the conversion of every person who decides for Christ. There is mystery at the birth of every child. We can understand aspects of biology, psychology, and sociology, but the beginning of new life has a core and source beyond our capacity to grasp and analyze fully. Such is the case with church renewal. There are skills to learn, methods to be added to our repertoire, and problem-solving techniques to develop. But at the heart of renewal lies mystery, a fact that must never be forgotten or factored out.

There are two temptations to be resisted at this point. One is to demand a how-to program. This temptation wants to know exactly what was done successfully somewhere else so that it can be tried at home. New England proved to be harsh soil for transplanting church growth programs. Big hit programs in other parts of the country failed miserably in New England. Instead, the growing churches used mostly home-grown methods, ideas, and approaches developed out of our particular context for our particular neighbors. Picking up new ideas is good, but they must not be viewed as the central solution for renewal.

The second temptation is to start to speak before you know what to say. When I was in high school, I was on a "College Bowl" type quiz show. I once pushed the buzzer on a question only to have my mind go blank. I had the attention of all the viewers but could just grin foolishly and silently into the camera. Before pastors and church leaders can speak and lead effectively for renewal, they must be clear about the message and goal for which they are responsible. I buzzed quickly because I thought I knew the answer, and it is easy to preach and plan programs before hearing from God. These two temptations—looking for how-tos and speaking before we have a message—must be resisted. Otherwise we are bound to take another lap around the field and end up at the same point of frustration over our dying churches.

To put first things first, then, vision is where we must start. Survival mentality is a disease of vision deficiency, so its cure lies in a restoration of vital, driving vision. The vision has to be clear and the visionary mind-set established before how-tos can be applied successfully. In fact, getting clear about the vision will answer many of the practical questions; emphases, priorities, and themes to focus on will be more readily apprehended. Clear vision takes care of the number of foundational decisions.

Part of the mystery of renewal is like the Gestalt switch: does a person see a picture of a vase or the silhouettes of two faces? Survival mentality churches see only the vase—the glorious past and the present problems. Renewal of vision is a switch of spiritual insight and perception that sees also the two faces—the possibilities for the future. Nothing has changed except the eye of the beholder. Recapturing vision is about that change.

The next three chapters will set forth a vision for renewal. They will trace the outline of the vision to aid the switch of perception. Some practical ideas and implications can be drawn from these chapters, but the focus will be on the content of the vision itself. Chapters 6 and 7 will be more practical, examining the ministry of the vision bearer who serves as midwife to the congregational new birth. The vision bearer has to be able to help others see the vision, to hear the message before proclaiming it, and to know the goal before leading the people forth.

The corporate vision of the church must cover three topics for renewal to occur: God, the church, and the world. Perceiving the vision and following it can be understood in terms of a journey. A journey has a destination that is clear to the traveler, but the way to the goal may be unknown and full of uncertainties. The image of a journey can be helpful in analyzing vision. Our church came to speak of a threefold journey: a journey upward of worship toward God, a journey inward of nurture toward one another, and a journey outward of mission toward the world.

Once the renewal began, the formulation of our vision evolved as we struggled to resolve our church identity crisis. We were no longer the old Dorchester Temple defined by the past; rather we were moving toward the future that God had in store for us. We lacked a clear sense of God's call, though we sensed it in bits and pieces. Through a process of prayer, preaching, study, and discussion, a new church covenant was made. It was in this process that the phraseology of the threefold journey was shaped.

Our formulation is certainly not the only one God can use to inspire a church. It grew out of our people and our situation. The expressions of other congregations may be very different. For just as we are all unique as individuals, so we are unique as gathered groups of God's people. In fact, there need not be a clear systematized formulation at all. The threefold journey concept was not developed until a couple years after the first breakout from survival mentality's grip. The vision and the ideas contained within it were present before its systematic expression. Whatever the form, the basic vision must be present. It may be in process, coming slowly into focus, but the kernel vision must be there. Just as the kingdom of God is like the mustard seed, starting so small yet becoming a large shrub to give refuge to the birds, so, too, vision may be small, but it grows and transforms those who behold it.

The rest of this chapter will outline the first component of the vision—the vision of God, the upward journey. Though each of these components of the threefold journey can be applied to the life of individual Christians, the focus here will be on the corporate journey, the vision of the church folks together.

Stunted Faith of Survival Mentality

Survival mentality is a spiritual condition rooted in unbelief. There is no vision for the future, no vision for mission, no vision for the growth of the congregation because the vision of who God is has been stunted. Though the church may have many individuals with sincere and deep personal faith in Christ, when they gather together and act as a body, they lose the transcendent element. God is a living, dynamic, ever-creative Spirit. Yet, there is little or nothing dynamic and creative in the dying church. The despair and fear of the members reveal their loss of faith.

It is human nature for individuals to be influenced by the accepted patterns of the group. When my family, which is widely scattered across the United States, gets together for reunions, it is easy to fall into the familiar patterns of relating that we established in our childhood. But we've all grown and changed over the years. We've abandoned many of our immature responses and have been healed of some of our brokenness. Still, when we get together, there is a pull toward patterns of the past. We deliberately have to choose to rise above them and create new patterns among us. When the individuals in a survivalist congregation gather together, there is seductive pull into unbelief. This unbelief can happen to even strong Christians. The forces of decline can only be resisted by a deliberate choice of faith to turn their eyes toward Jesus as one body. But survival mentality offers no vision of God to cause people to lift up their eyes and break out of old patterns. As they see all their problems, they feel helpless and even abandoned by God, though none would dare say it aloud. Their lack of faith is summed up in the cry of the psalmist: "Why dost thou stand afar off, O LORD? Why dost thou hide thyself in times of trouble?" (Psalm 10:1). It is hard to have vision when it feels as though God has abandoned you, as if God has moved to the suburbs like many former members; and with God goes the vision.

In a survivalist church the old forms and rituals linger on with comfortable familiarity. The worship life of the congregation is not a dynamic journey, but more like a static tableau recalling an earlier time of vitality. The hymns, liturgy, sermon styles, and the small habits of worship feel tired but are somewhat reassuring because they are known so well. The worship is like an old living room chair, a loved favorite spot. But to an outsider that chair can look like a piece of junk ready for the trash heap. The traditional forms and expressions of worship may appeal to the dwindling remnant, but to the new generation, to the shifting cultures in the surrounding neighborhood, the worship is alien and out of touch. The language of worship is bound to a culture of the past, so there is no reaching out to the world in their worship. Their services are an island rather than a bridge to bring people into the presence of God.

The God Who Is Present

Renewing the worship life of the church begins with a vision of God as present. Christ is the head of the body, his church. This is not merely a theological truth, but a dynamic reality. So renewal must begin by calling the Christians in survivalist churches to open their eyes to Christ's presence in their particular church. Jesus said, "And I, when I am lifted up from the earth, will draw all people to myself" (John 12:32, adapted). Jesus is inherently attractive. For people who have already made commitments of faith there is a deep longing to know God more fully, even if our lives as individuals and congregations often get bogged down or sidetracked. Through preaching, teaching, prayer, example, and conversation, the presence of Christ here and now needs to be lifted up.

As the presence of Christ is acknowledged, the Holy Spirit begins to work. The downward spiral of decline shifts to an upward spiral of faith. As Christ is recognized as the present head of the church, he is free to move in our lives. Answers to prayer are seen, which strengthens our faith to pray and labor with hope, which in turn leads to God's greater unleashing of power and creativity among us. The Psalms tell us, "Unless the LORD builds the house, those who build it labor in vain" (Psalm 127:1). The work of renewal is God's work. Our need is to have the spiritual eyes to behold it. As the Lord said to the prophet Isaiah, "Behold, I am doing a new thing; now it springs forth, do you not perceive it?" (Isaiah 43:19). Churches need to perceive the new things God is doing, and then they will have the vision to step out in faith, knowing that God is the ever-present creative inspirational leader of God's people.

The breakout from survival mentality by Dorchester Temple Baptist Church illustrates the interaction of the living Spirit of Christ with people responding to him with a faith-filled vision. After decades of decline, a foundation of visionary proclamation had been laid and many small steps taken to prepare the way for renewal. I had been preaching about God's call to the future, addressing renewal issues in board meetings and Bible study, and slowly winning the trust of folks in the congregation through pastoral visits and listening. A few new people had joined, drawn by the up-beat messages they heard. Some of the older members were voicing their affirmation and support for trying to look to the future. Some older members joined a Bible study group with some of the newer members, which sparked creative interaction between the two groups. But the congregation in its corporate experience was still survivalist. We needed a corporate conversion, a shared awakening to a vision of God.

A financial crisis was the opportunity to choose to rise above the old spiral of decline. Our pre-Advent pledge drive had failed miserably. We had received pledges for less than one-third of the proposed budget. Two deacons even told me to begin looking for another church to protect myself in case they couldn't support me. But instead of undertaking a panicky round of guilt-producing financial appeals, we held a prayer meeting on the first Friday in January 1980 to offer up our needs to the Lord. The need was approached not only in anxiety but also in fervent prayer by a significant number of the remnant people and newcomers. The answer to our prayers was not long in coming.

The following Sunday I was going to preach on 2 Chronicles 7:14: "If my people who are called by my name humble themselves, and pray and seek my face, and turn from their wicked ways, then I will hear from heaven, and will forgive their sin and heal their land." The message was basically that this was God's church—not the old members' church or the newcomers' church, not the whites' church or the blacks' church, not the deacons' church or the pastor's church. This was God's church, and we had better let God do whatever God wanted to do with it. If we opened ourselves to God, the Lord would take care of all our difficulties. I knew I was going to preach on that subject, but nobody else did.

Just as I was about to go into the service, one of our elderly deacons approached me all distraught and in tears. He had seen something while coming to church on the bus that had deeply upset him. We prayed for a brief moment before proceeding on into the service. Meanwhile, our pianist had decided to scrap the normal prelude and, without consulting with me, began to lead the congregation in choruses. As I came into the sanctuary, an atmosphere of worship and expectation was already growing. Part way through the service the old deacon stood up and said, "I came into church today all upset, but Jesus has ministered to me and lifted my burden. I want us all to sing 'Now I Belong to Jesus.' " Our congregation was not used to such spontaneity. We had always diligently followed the printed order of worship, but now we sang the requested song of testimony. There were a number of other small incidents of unplanned worship, which the congregation sensed were Spirit-led. By the time I got up to preach my sermon, God had already illustrated it for me. We all experienced the dynamic presence of the risen Lord as head of this particular part of his body.

After a time of confession, we closed with a celebration of the Lord's Supper. At the end of the service many older members were in tears. One deacon said, "I don't know what's happening, but it's good." What was happening was the birth of a new vision of God, a renewal of faith in Christ at work among us. We knew without a shadow of doubt that God was alive, that Christ was still the head of the church, that the Spirit would move and direct the gathered people of God. All those present at that service point back to it as the moment when our survivalist thinking was shattered by the renewal of our corporate spirit. We were commencing a new journey together from that point, an upward journey inspired by new faith in the living God present among us.

Nobody can plan or program such an event. It is God's

doing, which is precisely why faith placed in God is awakened. The building of this house must be God's work. God is the owner and contractor. We each labor and have our proper tasks and roles, but in the final analysis it is the moving of God that brings the whole project together.

The early church expected God to be active in their life together, including the points of crisis. In Acts 4, Peter and John have just been given a gag order by the same people who had crucified Jesus. They went back to the other believers, and everyone prayed. Acts 4:31 tells of the climax of their meeting: "When they had prayed, the place in which they were gathered together was shaken; and they were all filled with the Holy Spirit and spoke the word of God with boldness." The initial role of Christians was to present themselves in prayer before God, to pray, and to wait. Then it was God who acted, pouring out the Holy Spirit in such a way that the believers knew God was sovereign and would uphold them in the coming conflict. Instead of being intimidated, they were inspired to greater boldness in proclaiming Christ.

The upward journey of worship begins as we wait upon God in prayer and worship. God still acts today in the church in ways such that the entire gathered group can discern the moving of the Spirit. Sometimes things get shaken metaphorically as well as literally. The old familiar patterns, the comfortable rituals, and the complacency that often accommodate decline will be shaken. The new wine of the gospel tends to burst old wineskins. But the outcome is renewed vision, clearer direction, and energized faith.

The church that would break out of survival mentality needs to go back to its foundations, back to the cross and the empty tomb of Jesus, and take a serious look at who their Lord really is. They need to make the commitment to pray together. The praying of the church must be more than the sparsely attended midweek prayer meeting, if that particular format has survived amid the decline. Individuals must be committed to private prayer on behalf of God's work for renewal. Groups that gather for purposes of Bible study or church business need to give focused time to prayer for renewal. There must be a commitment to pray by enough people to affect the spirit of the whole congregation. The sincere seeking of God is the first step of the upward journey. And God honors that step of faith. Just gathering together to pray takes faith. It is a step out of the fear that characterizes survival mentality. It is a step of vision, trusting that God is really there to hear and answer our prayers. "Whoever would draw near to God must believe that he exists and that he rewards those who seek him" (Hebrews 11:6).

How does the congregation break the grip of survivalism enough to take that step of prayer? This is a mystery of God's grace, just as the birth of faith in a human heart is shrouded in mystery. The way must be prepared. Christ can be lifted up through preaching and teaching, but God is the one who ignites the spark, both in urging people to pray and in moving the Spirit to respond. We need to be reminded again and again that the work is God's work and that God is perfectly capable to do it. Eventually we will begin to believe what we have been verbally affirming all along. Then the journey has begun, the vision is beginning to dawn.

The Growing Vision

Renewal doesn't happen in one service or one revival. It is an ongoing process. A wedding isn't a marriage; it is only the beginning of a marriage. A new state is entered into with new commitments, new horizons, new challenges for growth. A great wedding can be followed by a lousy marriage, so it is critical to nurture the relationship throughout the day-by-day routines of married life and build upon the vows made on the wedding day.

Once the church breaks out of the psychological vice of survival mentality and has caught a vision of God, it must journey onward in the energy of that new vision. It can't take one step and then quit with the glowing claim of accomplishment. The insights and hope of the breakthrough need to nurture the weekly routines of church life, from worship services to committee meetings. The upward journey must be deliberately pursued once the door to renewal is cracked open.

There needs to be a congregational hungering after God, thirsting for the living waters of Christ. The psalmist prayed: "As a hart longs for flowing streams, so longs my soul for thee, O God. My soul thirsts for God, for the living God" (Psalm 42:1-2). If this prayer echoes within the hearts of the folks in church, then seeking after God will become a part of their spirituality. The members will be quick to pray together, and their praying will not be mere formality but will be a deep expression of their spirits.

Jesus promised to satisfy those who hunger and thirst for him: "I am the bread of life; the one who comes to me shall not hunger, and the one who believes in me shall never thirst" (John 6:35, adapted). A hungry church, a praying church will know the continual, dynamic presence of God in their life together. And though satisfied in the sense of having their current needs met, a further hunger is triggered. Their appetites are whetted to grow more and more in their walk with Christ. As C. S. Lewis put it in *The Narnia Chronicles,* they will long to "go further up and further in."[1] The first steps of faith become a lifestyle of journeying toward God.

This journeying can be deliberately encouraged by developing the times of group prayer for the congregation. Pastoral prayers can be opened up to include prayers from the rest of the gathered worshipers. Committee and board meetings can begin and end with an extended period of open prayer rather than just a formalized prayer that often becomes

[1]C.S. Lewis, *The Last Battle* (London: Bodley Head, Ltd., 1956), p. 172.

merely a Christianized way of calling the meeting to order or adjourning it. In such moments of prayer the members of the committee can take the time to get spiritually centered and realize that they are really about God's business. Not only will such prayer result in more accepting attitudes toward one another, but the Spirit will have more access to our hearts and minds because we've taken time to listen as well as talk.

The church will have to wrestle again and again with what it means for Jesus to be Lord of the church. Survival mentality is afraid of losing control. But with a renewed vision of God, control must be relinquished by each person, including the pastor and other church leaders. Everyone has his or her pet projects, key priorities, and favorite missions in the church. But these must all be laid aside. We need to keep reminding one another that Christ is the head of the church. He sets the priorities and direction. Of course, everyone theoretically says that, but these aren't just pious statements masking normal human processes. The Spirit of God directs the people of God through a process of seeking, praying, discovering gifts, sharing burdens, and coming to consensus. It is an organic process, but it won't work if anyone is trying to use power politics to assert a personal agenda. With prayer, teaching, modeling, and feedback, people can learn to listen to the direction of the Spirit so that they can journey together under the Lord's guiding hand. Leadership that is responsive to Christ's direction through the whole body will have an authority rooted, not in themselves, but in Christ who has set forth the agenda that all have perceived.

Christ's direction can be recognized and responded to in the worship services. Certain dynamics are indicators of the Spirit's active presence in a congregation. The worship is highly participatory; many people use their spiritual gifts, express their prayers, and share their needs and testimonies (see 1 Corinthians 14:26). This can be done in a wide variety of forms, traditions, rituals, and opportunities for spontaneity, but the key is that people are participants in, not spectators of, the worship. Though the members may grapple with difficult issues, there is a strong drive toward consensus (see Acts 4:32). The people have a unity in their common commitment to Christ that explicitly and experientially supersedes all other values and agenda (see Ephesians 4:3-4). In group meetings for worship and business, a flow of emotion, need, and divine response can be discerned. This requires listening to what people are saying and to the feelings behind their words (or their silence) as well as listening to God's "still small voice" within to address those feelings. Leaders and even an entire congregation can be trained to practice these dynamics. Specific teaching can be accompanied by examples identified as they are happening. In a small informal worship group I would stop our worship when we were getting into the rut of singing our favorite choruses and songs and losing our purposes of the adoration of God. Richer worship almost always followed, for people responded with more focused attention. One Sunday I had prepared a rather upbeat sermon only to hear a number of parishioners expressing deep anguish over events in their lives that week. Their experiences set the tone for our service, and my sermon would have been irrelevant for them at that particular point. So I saved it for a more appropriate Sunday and spoke more briefly and spontaneously on the issues at hand, telling them what I was doing and why. Such a departure from my preparations was rare, but one must be sensitive and ready to respond to the present step in the congregation's journey if they are to experience God speaking to them. My explanation also enabled people to perceive the dynamic of the service and not just unconsciously experience the spiritual flow within the worship. At other times my sermon couldn't have been set up better by the spontaneous expressions of prayer or sharing during the service. As an introduction to the sermon, I would point out what people were saying and how God was addressing our concerns so that people would not just hear the Word of God but also understand how the Spirit had moved among us corporately that day. Like learning to ride a bike, the process of congregational discernment may be a bit awkward at first, but eventually being open to the Spirit's moving through all the people gathered together becomes a corporate skill.

Letting Christ creatively enter into our decision making is not automatic either, especially for survivalist churches, but it can be learned. My own tendency is to plan programs to answer any problematic situation. Sometimes they work; sometimes they don't. Much of the time what I propose or do is perceived as *my* project, and, in fact, I conceived it through my own process of problem solving with a prayer for God's blessing tacked on. After many failures, I began to learn to listen, and our congregation began to learn to listen. We each spoke about what was on our hearts, then we listened to what had been said to us all. Answers and direction began to emerge that were discerned by most of the people in the church, similar to the testimony in Acts that the believers were all "with one accord" (Acts 1:14). The result was that our undertakings were no longer *my* project, but a shared response to what we felt was the leading of the Lord. We have often verbally proclaimed that the Lord leads, but we seem to be surprised when it really works that way. Once the vision of God being present is renewed, folks are more willing to take the risk that God will lead. Finding and shaping our future then becomes an adventure rather than an intimidating nightmare.

We experienced the impact of the vision of God in our decision-making process during a series of meetings to deal with a leaky roof. This was the first major decision we had to make following the renewal experience of January 1980. After going through the initial process of getting bids for the new roof, all of which seemed beyond our means, one member raised the issue of insulating our entire roof. With the escalating cost of heating oil during those years, there couldn't have been a more opportune moment to do the job; but if the roof repair itself was going to take us beyond our limits financially, insulating the roof seemed an impossibility, however necessary it might be. The initial congregational business meeting was a heated one as people debated the wisdom and fiscal practicality of insulating the roof. A deadlock developed, and it was decided to meet again in two weeks. During the interim the church board was to study the situation more fully and come up with firmer cost estimates and oil savings estimates. Furthermore, everyone agreed to pray individually as well as together.

Two weeks later the dollar figures were still the same, but the attitude of the congregation was different. One longtime member spoke up, "God has never let us down when we've stepped out in faith." The new vision of God being dynamically present among us was being applied to our mundane financial decisions. Others made similar statements, and it was voted to do the job and trust God to move among us to raise the money. Then an older woman offered to make a no-interest long-term loan to the church for the unfinanced balance. Her generous offer was inspired by the faith of the people in God's active care and leading of the congregation. Our business meeting adjourned with people crying, hugging, and singing praises. Our emotions were triggered, not because of the issue on the agenda, but because we had felt the temptation of survivalism and despair and had together affirmed and acted upon the vision of God being with us.

In the process of growing in the vision of God, there will be many stumbles and false steps. Old patterns and habits don't disappear at the breakthrough points, just as our old sins didn't evaporate when we accepted Christ. There is an ever-present need to accept the grace of Christ upon our journey. The work of confession and repentance needs to be done periodically and done, not only as individuals, but as a church. At a number of key points, with the help of thoughtful feedback from some members, I confronted the congregation with our sinful or unbelieving attitudes which were bogging us down. We named them specifically so that they wouldn't be able to lurk around in the dark backstages of our consciousness and relationships. We confronted racism, dissension, self-righteousness, apathy, and other attitudes when they seemed to creep into the life of our whole body.

While attending a conference, I was convicted of some specific sins in my life that were affecting my ministry: pride, hyperactivity, doing work in my own strength. I set aside my planned sermon and preached on Hebrews 12:1-4, calling us all to "lay aside every weight, and sin which clings so closely." I confessed my sins, not hiding behind their generalities, but illustrating specifically how they worked in me and therefore affected others. I asked for forgiveness and waited till the congregation responded. Then I challenged them, addressing attitudes of indifference toward the children in the church, our privitization, and our decision-making process as a church. All these were holding us back from following God more faithfully as a church. Another time I spoke about racism. We had prided ourselves on our inclusivity, so I showed explicitly how we were still divided and how racism still was entwined in our church life. Such blunt confrontation was not done often, and I exposed these sins in a confessional way rather than in a condemning fashion. Jesus said the Spirit would "convict the world of guilt in regard to sin" (John 16:8, NIV), and so as we confessed, we felt corporately the Spirit's work among us.

Each time we confessed and repented of these sins as a people, we found a deepening of our unity and spiritual vitality. Fresh streams of compassion flowed between us. We found new energy to minister to one another and reach out to our neighborhood. It wasn't easy to face our distorted attitudes openly and bluntly, but we could do it in the context of God's grace. We were given the freedom of being accepted right where we were, so we did not need to protect ourselves and hide in fear like the survivalist. Instead we had a vision of God present in grace with power to forgive and renew. With such a vision the people flourish.

The Vision of the Church

*T*he second aspect of the threefold journey is a journey inward, a journey inspired by a vision of the church. Dr. Gordon Fee describes a Christian as someone who is trying to become what they already are in Christ. A church may be defined similarly: a group of believers trying to become what they already are in Christ. We are the body of Christ. Our inward journey as a church is to become more fully that body of Christ, to grow up into full maturity, to actualize that spiritual reality in our corporate life to a greater degree than ever before.

The Stunted Ecclesiology of Survival Mentality

Just as survival mentality's vision of God is pathetically stunted, so is the vision of the church. Instead of seeking to actualize the potential of the gospel to ever greater degrees, the survivalist church is retreating in fear from a host of problems and doubts and fears. Biblical images may be used in the pulpit and classrooms, but they are not operative in the group psychology. They do not direct and shape the formation of the church. Instead a number of unconscious and unbiblical images become the operative ones. They are unnamed, but they are felt and acted upon. To name them is to shame them, for each image is tragically incomplete and distorted, leading to the crippling of Christ's body. These images each contain a bit of truth, a bit of what needs to be incorporated into a proper vision, but taken by themselves, these images become narrow, limiting, and even destructive.

The first image is of a club. People gather together to be with other like-minded folks and have a good time. Of course, a good time is defined in terms of religious activities, but the members gather mainly for their own sake and benefit.

The second image is closely related—that of a massage parlor. The church is a place to come and receive comfort, to be made to feel good. Rather than addressing difficult issues of the decline or changes in the community, the church is where you go to get away from it all. Let go of your troubles, not by letting Christ bear the burdens with you, but by pretending they are not there.

The third image is what happens when fear intrudes upon the club or massage parlor. Then the church becomes the Alamo, an outpost surrounded by a threatening and hostile world. The neighborhood experiences population shifts, so there are people of different color or nationality all around. The physiological wagons are pulled into a circle, and the defenses go up. As our church was going through transition, one older woman actually told me, "Dorchester Temple was never meant to be a colored church!" Her fear and bigotry revealed a vision of the church as an enclave being invaded. I wasn't manning my post to keep the church secure. The walls of our spiritual Alamo were being breached.

In a different vein, the church may be viewed as a theater that specializes in the old classics. There is a successful movie theater north of Boston that runs only old movies, the classics of a few years back. People pay because they know what they are getting; they have seen most of these films before and liked them. The church sticks with the classics according to its particular tradition. There is a lot of good in the classic expressions of our faith. But the result of this image is that the church lives in an era that is long gone. It

becomes out of touch with the present. It is no longer powerful and pertinent, merely interesting to those who like that
era. It is a spiritualized form of the same nostalgia that plays
fifties rock 'n' roll and watches "Leave It to Beaver" reruns.

A similar image is that of the museum—a place to preserve the memories. It houses memories of baptisms and
weddings, funerals and fellowship events, family ties and
friendships. Memorial plaques record the family names as-
sociated with this picture, that pew, this window, that tro-
phy case. Most of the people are scattered, and the remain-
ing members are curators of the memories.

The current members of survivalist churches live too close
to the realities of the decline with its shrinking membership
and shriveling finances. The image of a failing business
haunts them. It is a cold image, a stark one, but it dominates
much of their psyche and decisions. It calls forth the desire
to grasp control and use the techniques of guilt to keep
afloat. If they don't hold it together, the corporation will go
bankrupt.

The final image is the most prophetic one, that of a nurs-
ing home. The church becomes a haven for a few elderly
folks until they pass on and the church finally dies with
them. Pastors are there on a part-time basis, if at all, to visit
and comfort them in their final days. Since we do not believe
in mercy killing, we let churches linger on, dying in slow
agony. Even denominations can mentally shut out churches
in such advance stages of decline much like the warehousing
of the frail elderly. Death is ugly, and dying churches are not
nice to look at either.

A Vision of the Reconciled Body of Christ

Fortunately, Jesus is not in the business of mercy killing
either, but rather that of healing and resurrection. These
inadequate and harmful images can be washed away by the
surging of a renewed vision of the church. Renewed vision

of God leads into a renewed vision of the church. As our faith is awakened, the images that grow out of fear and despair are replaced by images of growth and hope.

The major biblical image of the church is of the reconciled body of Christ. Paul's theology of the church is the most developed in the Scriptures. In 1 Corinthians 12:12-13, he states, "For just as the body is one and has many members, and all the members of the body though many, are one body, so it is with Christ. For by one Spirit we were all baptized into one body—Jews or Greeks, slaves or free—and all were made to drink of one Spirit." The image of a human body is applied to the church. We are together Christ's body, the physical expression of who Jesus is in the world. Christ is the head (Ephesians 4:15), and his life animates and energizes the whole body.

It is absolutely fundamental, then, for the body to be healthy, that its various parts be in harmony. Christ's body is a reconciled body. All believers, whatever their background, culture, language, or sex, are incorporated into one body. Human distinctions are broken down. Paul is clear in his vision: "There is neither Jew nor Greek, there is neither slave nor free, there is neither male nor female; for you are all one in Christ Jesus" (Galatians 3:28). "Here there cannot be Greek and Jew, circumcised and uncircumcised, barbarian, Scythian, slave, free, but Christ is all, and in all" (Colossians 3:11, adapted). Any concept of the church that sees the church as Christ's body must be inclusive, for Christ as head has made his body an inclusive one for all who believe.

To undercut the inclusive nature of the church, to deny participation to a segment of believers, is to attack the cross of Christ itself. In Ephesians 2, after expressing the marvel of being saved by grace through faith and being made alive in Christ, Paul goes on to show that the cross is not just a place of reconciliation between God and individuals. There is a horizontal element that makes peace and forges reconciliation among all Christians.

Therefore remember that at one time you Gentiles in the flesh, called uncircumcision by what is called the circumcision, which is made in the flesh by hands—remember that you were at that time separated from Christ, alienated from the commonwealth of Israel, and strangers to the covenants of promise, having no hope and without God in the world. But now in Christ Jesus you who once were far off have been brought near in the blood of Christ. For he is our peace, who has made us both one, and has broken down the dividing wall of hostility, by abolishing in his flesh the law of commandments and ordinances, that he might create in himself one new humanity in place of the two, so making peace, and might reconcile us both to God in one body through the cross, thereby bringing the hostility to an end. And he came and preached peace to you who were far off and peace to those who were near; for through him we both have access in one Spirit to the Father. So then you are no longer strangers and sojourners, but you are fellow citizens with the saints and members of the household of God, built upon the foundation of the apostles and prophets, Christ Jesus himself being the cornerstone, in whom the whole structure is joined together and grows into a holy temple in the Lord; in whom you also are built into it for a dwelling place of God in the Spirit (Ephesians 2:11-22, adapted).

Any church that sets up dividing walls explicitly or implicitly is undoing the reconciling work of the Lord Jesus upon the cross. It is in a grave state of spiritual rebellion, living in practical heresy. It is abandoning the very central element that makes a true church of Christ.

The vision of heaven is of "a great multitude which no one could number, from every nation, from all tribes and peoples and tongues" (Revelation 7:9, adapted). That is the picture of the church triumphant; and if God's will is to be done on earth as it is in heaven, it must be the picture of the church militant, the church still in the midst of this age.

Practically speaking, we must welcome any who would come, from whatever race, nationality, class, or generation. Welcome includes acceptance, letting people be fully themselves. When blacks join predominantly white churches, they should not be expected to leave their black heritage and culture to fit into an all-white setting. To expect any people to subordinate their cultural distinctives to the dominant culture is not to extend acceptance and therefore not to allow true reconciliation to take place. The Jew and Greek don't give up their Jewishness or Greekness to come to Christ. Rather, they don't let their different identities remain a barrier between them. To use the body analogy, the ears and hands don't demand that the other become like themselves. Each organ with its own unique form and function has a place within the whole and needs the other organs to be fully themselves if the body is to be strong and healthy. Genuine acceptance means each person has to allow those who are different to be fully themselves.

After all, the common bond between people in the church is Christ. Family ties, national heritage, race, sex, age—all are of no significance as a bond in Christ's body. Jesus Christ is the hub of the wheel holding together the spokes that come from a variety of directions. It is the presence of the living Christ in human hearts that establishes our bonding in the church. Throughout Dorchester Temple's transition this has been made evident. For many of those who left, the church was a web of social ties, family relationships, and certain ways of worship. What the church meant to them was fading away in the decline; and it also would diminish in renewal, for new ties and patterns would develop. As a result, what the church meant to them was no more, so they left. The people who stayed, however, had to adjust to cultural changes, new styles, and different social ties; but they could make the transition because for them the person of the living Christ was central. They could recognize him through many different forms.

Music is perhaps the clearest example to watch diversity develop within the oneness of Christ. The classical hymns and revival songs that are the musical bread and butter of most Baptist churches have a rich treasure of theological and experiential expression. Contemporary folk and gospel music is also very Christ-centered, though in completely different musical forms. To accept one another in Christ, people from different backgrounds need to recognize Christ in music that is different from that with which they identify, not in a paternalistic fashion, but with humility that seeks to learn more of Christ. Each musical language can express the glories of the gospel differently. Just as our portrait of Christ is enriched by four gospels, so our musical portrait of Christ is enriched by expressions in styles from classical to jazz to gospel. An inclusive church will look primarily not at the style but at Christ in the musical medium. The familiar musical language needs to be used, but different forms, if used with openness and respect, can open up new insights and experiences of Christ. People in older traditions can learn to appreciate newer choruses and Scripture songs. People who grew up on rock 'n' roll can discover the riches of the hymns they once thought were musty and boring. The key is acceptance of the different cultures by virtue of recognizing Christ in each.

To lift up effectively the vision of the church as the reconciled body of Christ, racism, ethnocentrism, ageism and other exclusive prejudices must be exposed as sin. The exclusive "isms" can be preached about, illustrated both from the Bible and from specific instances in the congregational life. They are hideous blemishes on the body of Christ. Pious talk about oneness in Christ is of no value if the roots of prejudice aren't pulled out. They are weeds in the garden of God that will choke out the harvest God wants to produce. When these weeds of prejudice creep up in conversations or meetings, they must directly, gently, yet firmly be countered. The pastor can take a lead, but other members will need to bear the responsibility of turning aside from the ways of prejudice as well. Many survivalist churches are ethnically pure islands in changing neighborhoods, and there will be no renewal until the congregation is willing to welcome people who are different, not only to fill pews and give money but to shape worship, ministry, and make decisions that reflect the new culture as well as the old one. In some communities that will mean being open to different ethnic groups, but it will also mean opening up to younger people of a different generation or people who grew up outside of the church and bring very different assumptions with them now that they have made commitments of faith.

A new identity can be nurtured that is based not on cultural or blood ties but on faith ties. The Bible uses words like "chosen race" and "God's own people" to speak of the new corporate identity in Christ (1 Peter 2:9). The terms of family life are brought into the church, and Christians call each brothers and sisters (James 2:15). The reconciled church then seeks to build ties beyond culture, ties centered in Christ. They will work to get to know one another as individuals, seeking to understand their uniqueness and the cultural context which has helped shape them. The ministry of hospitality when practiced thoroughly in the church can forge new bonds of love and support that will be deeper and more profound than the bonds of culture or even earthly families.

Welcoming new people and new cultures into a church is not easy, but reconciliation never is. The word "reconciliation" indicates that there are issues that need to be worked out, gulfs to be bridged, barriers to be overcome. If a church has a vision of itself as the reconciled body of Christ, then it would be willing to take the risks and make the effort to forge a new community. It is significant that the followers of Jesus were first called Christians in Antioch (Acts 11:26), for the church there bridged the gap between Jews and Gentiles. They built a cosmopolitan church whose very nature and makeup testified to Christ as their only common bond.

Presenting All as Mature in Christ

The goal of the reconciled body of Christ is to present every person as mature in Christ. As the human body grows, each organ and member grows at the proper rate so that they all reach maturity together. If one organ doesn't grow, a serious health problem develops. Stunted growth of members in Christ's body decreases the spiritual health of the church. The goal is to enable all to grow and reach their God-given potential as children of God. Paul said of his own ministry, "Him we proclaim, warning every person and teaching every person in all wisdom, that we may present every person mature in Christ" (Colossians 1:28, adapted).

The work of the church, then, is to nurture spiritual growth, to help parent each of us in the process of becoming a fully mature disciple of Christ. Every member needs to be challenged to grow, for none of us can ever claim we have arrived. Too many churchgoers become complacent about spiritual growth. They feel what they learned as children in Sunday school is sufficient to last for a lifetime. The renewed vision of the church challenges that assumption; it challenges people to begin a lifelong journey of discipleship. Spiritual growth is for everyone from 1 to 101. There are no retirees.

We began with a yearlong Bible study course which I drew up called "Living the Christian Adventure." Our Wednesday night Bible study group worked through it one year, and the next year it was taken up by the adult Sunday school class. This foundational study of Christian discipleship covered our relationship to God, nurturing that relationship, life in the church, and living faithfully in the world. Then, as more people were interested in study, more groups were formed. One was a women's support group that nurtured the members in their personal struggles and rooted them deeply in Bible study and prayer. Other groups did systematic studies of the books of the Bible and prayed for one another. Groups could be formed according to common needs or to build community around a common discipline of study. The resources available through denominations and Christian book stores offer limitless possibilities for small groups, and creative leaders can custom make study programs for use with the particular groups that they lead. The underlying assumption to be cultivated in all these settings is that our lives are a constant journey toward Christ and wholeness, and God has much to say to direct, enable, and sustain us for that journey.

With a vision of growth, the life of the church is energized, for the people will be energized. Arthur was a retired man who had been in church most of his life but knew little of the Bible. When he caught the vision of spiritual growth, he became an avid Bible reader, joined our Wednesday night group, then worked at integrating what he learned into his life. A few years later as Arthur was dying of cancer, he feebly spoke to me from his hospital bed, "I'm still growing, aren't I?" He was a man who caught the vision for spiritual growth, and as a result, he played a key role in revitalizing the church as a whole.

Besides growing, the vision of maturity encompasses working. Children grow physically, but they also develop their skills in using tools, working with their hands and minds. Their coming to maturity will be reflected in undertaking a vocation, a life work. Each person in the church has a ministry, a calling. The nurturing church helps people discover those calls and develop the gifts to fulfill their ministries. The church must embrace a vision of job training. Many survivalist churches are going backwards in that they have fewer and fewer people doing the work. In spite of all the complaints about how others aren't pulling their weight, the overloaded leaders often are unwilling to train others to take over their responsibilities. The fear that nobody can do it as well as they can and that everything will collapse if they leave keeps them holding on to control. The renewed vision of the church will turn this around. Ways will be explored to help people try out their gifts. If they fail occasionally, they will be encouraged to go back and try again.

Our homegrown course, "Living the Christian Adventure," included a major section on spiritual gifts. We studied gifts and ministries in the Bible and then worked as a group to help one another discover and refine our understanding of our own gifts and God's call for us to be ministers. To drive the point home, the front of our bulletin stated:

Ministers: the entire congregation
Pastor: Rev. Daniel L. Buttry

I borrowed this idea from another church, but it helped us clarify our call and identity, too. Some of our youth participated in Youth Leader Corp, a discipleship and training program run by our state denominational youth ministry. These teens deepened their Christian commitment, discovered their gifts, and were put into positions of leadership where they could minister as they felt called. One young woman became a regular worship leader, displaying more giftedness in that capacity than some of our seminarians!

If gifts are discovered and put to use, the range of ministry and level of excitement in the church will dramatically increase. Work has great value to us. We were created by God to work, to be caretakers of the garden. So it is inherent in who we are to give of ourselves to create and produce in some fashion. A church that fosters and encourages all persons to discover and use their gifts will be a church that will give people the opportunity to mature as workers with God.

No church will ever arrive at the point of perfection in this life. There will always be problems, struggles, and failures to be dealt with. Survival mentality churches let the problems, struggles, and failures dictate the terms of their life together. Churches who have caught a renewed vision of themselves as the reconciled body of Christ will let the vision of God's future set the terms of their life together. They will always be striving to become what they already are in Christ.

Dorchester Temple closes its Communion service by forming a circle around the edges of the sanctuary to sing

"Blest Be the Tie That Binds." The practice began before my pastorate, and when I first came, it seemed a sharply prophetic contrast to what existed. There were some serious racist attitudes; newcomers were viewed with suspicion. The tie that binds was pretty loose. But we kept singing it, for that song expresses the truth of what we are to be as a church. As we grew and experienced more reconciliation, the circle broadened, and people from many racial, ethnic, and class backgrounds joined hands with us. More and more, our singing began to express what was happening among us. There were still areas of discord, stress points in our unity, major lacks in our compassion. But the hymn became a celebration of what God had done and a call to mature even further. We had caught a vision of what it meant to be the church, a vision of a journey of nurture, striving together to become mature in Christ. Guided by that vision, Dorchester Temple is now on the way.

The Vision of Mission

*T*he third aspect of the threefold journey is a journey outward of mission
toward the world. Christians are called to be ambassadors
for Christ, so there needs to be a clear idea of what it means
to properly represent Christ in the world.

The Stunted Mission of Survival Mentality

Survivors can't see much beyond themselves. All their
energy and concentration is taken up in matters of hanging
on from week to week. A church in survival mentality is
bound to have a stunted mission because this mind-set is
inherently inward. The goal is to keep the doors open rather
than extending the involvement and impact of the church
into every corner of the neighborhood. The ambassadors for
Christ in survivalist churches are holed up in the security of
their embassy compound when they should be entering into
the surrounding society, making new friends for the One
who sent them. Survivalist churches are on the defensive,
and their stunted mission reflects that defensive posture.

Evangelism is not seen as fishing for people, going out to
where the folks are and bearing witness of Christ to them;
instead evangelism becomes a feeble hope that people will
somehow stumble into the church and be brought to faith
by what they see and hear. Such a hope is almost never
fulfilled because those who do drop in usually see what is

really there: a dying and depressed church which is certainly not good news of great joy! The survivalist church puts all its evangelistic eggs in the basket of visitors dropping in, and they seldom hatch.

Where there is an occasional success in evangelism, there is not much hope of longer-term discipleship and Christian development. Genuine new converts come with a great deal of zeal and often with fresh, if untried, ideas. They are eager to share their faith with their friends. Such enthusiasm and new blood is threatening to survival mentality since it brings change. On the one hand, the older church members want new members, but on the other, they want to maintain the cherished ways and the tight-knit circles of relationships. Far too often whatever initial success is made in transforming lives with the gospel is undone by reluctance to change. The new wine bursts the skins and the wine is lost, though the skins of survivalist churches have an amazing capacity to weather the loss of new wine. I have observed churches go through periodic cycles of gradual infusion of newcomers who then get squeezed out by the dominant core that is afraid of change. One Dorchester church was experiencing modest growth until a power clash developed which resulted in the pastor resigning and most of the new members leaving. A few years later new members began to trickle in again, but once more the people in power were unwilling to accommodate new ideas and concerns. The church was torn apart with lawsuits, and the internal battle received major press coverage. Each time through the cycle leaves the church more calcified and less likely to respond to new opportunities.

The church is sent into the world by Christ, but survivalist churches are not interested in going out of themselves into the world of problems and disturbing people. A survivalist church has a mission-compound mentality. It is surrounded by a hostile culture, an alien people, so a safe haven is set up with high protective walls. Some urban churches have even taken this mental state and incarnated it. There is a church in Dorchester surrounded by an eight-foot chain link fence. Fear of vandalism has made a physical and mental prison into which the church has locked itself. No mission will happen through that church until the physical and mental fences come down.

The people outside the church may be threatening, too. Sometimes they are of a different race. Dorchester Temple was once made up of Yankee and Canadian Baptists, a reflection of the neighborhood in the 1920s to 1940s. But then Irish Catholics began moving in from the east and blacks from the north. There was some deep prejudice toward people in both these groups, so little effort was made to reach out to these new neighbors. As the initial population group from the church declined in the neighborhood, church membership also plummeted. Sometimes the needs of people outside the church are too threatening. A pastor of one small declining church began reaching out to deinstitutionalized people in his city, people with deep and complex emotional needs, people who didn't act "proper." They joined the adult Sunday school class where they sometimes made inappropriate comments, but they were growing in their understanding of God's love for them. One deacon, however, directly criticized the pastor for bringing "riffraff" into the church. To deal with such needy people would shake up a lot of comfortable patterns in that church, and this deacon was unwilling to make that sacrifice.

The survivalist church may be able to pride itself on what it does for missions at a distance. They may get on the missions speaker circuit and support denominational and faith missions. However, their foreign mission involvement is, in contemporary terms, a cop-out. They are sending dollars overseas but ignoring their task at hand. They support Bible translation for jungle tribes but refuse to translate their faith and worship into the cultural languages and forms that abound in their own society. They pay for others to go into all the world but personally refuse to go into their own neighborhood. Their mission involvement has become mercenary. They pay someone else to do what they themselves will not do. Genuine foreign mission needs to surge out of a passion for taking Christ to all the world, from my doorstep to the ends of the earth.

Behind the lack of outreach is an abandonment of the basic mission Jesus Christ gave to the church. He told his disciples to "go . . . and make disciples of all nations" (Matthew 28:19), but instead the survivalist churches have substituted a vision of self-gratification. What is comfortable and familiar is more important than reaching a changing and confusing world with the gospel of Christ. In focusing on their own survival and not on their responsibility as Christ's ambassadors to the world, these churches have forfeited their place in advancing God's kingdom. The warning of the risen Christ to the church at Laodicea needs to be heard and heeded:

> "I know your works: you are neither cold nor hot. Would that you were cold or hot! So, because you are lukewarm, and neither cold nor hot, I will spew you out of my mouth. For you say, I am rich, I have prospered, and I need nothing; not knowing that you are wretched, pitiable, poor, blind, and naked. Therefore I counsel you to buy from me gold refined by fire, that you may be rich, and white garments to clothe you and to keep the shame of your nakedness from being seen, and salve to anoint your eyes, that you may see. Those who I love, I reprove and chasten; so be zealous and repent" (Revelation 3:15-19).

The judgment is harsh, but we must face how dishonoring lukewarmness is to Jesus Christ.

Being Missionary Churches

Every local church must recognize that it is a missionary church. Our vision for mission needs to be reborn. The task of evangelism is not done. Justice and righteousness have not been established. Brokenness and heartache still abound. No church, whatever its location, can presume to be done with its mission work, only needing to keep the flock happy till the Lord calls them home. The need is all around. What is lacking is the vision to see the need, the vision to embrace the need as the call of Christ.

Every church is a missionary church. That means that rather than living out an image of a mission compound, we must be bridges into the surrounding society. Just as God took on human flesh and came into the world in Jesus Christ, we must leave the safety of our sanctuaries and enter into the world to do the work that Christ did. Our risen Lord said, "As the Father has sent me, even so I send you" (John 20:21). The ministers of the church are the entire congregation. The missionaries should also be the entire congregation. All of us are sent by Christ into the world to do mission work.

The effort foreign missionaries make to learn a new language and enter into a vastly different culture needs to be mirrored by a similar effort within our communities. We need to speak in the languages of our neighbors, not just verbally, but musically, artistically, and with compassion and concern for where people live. For example, evangelism dependent upon musical styles of nineteenth-century revivals and preaching that is white in style and theology will not get much hearing in black, urban neighborhoods. A church with a vision for mission in a changing or mixed community will speak the universal gospel in the forms that people will listen to and identify with. Our church has done street meetings using a jazz-rock-gospel sound. We showed films using rap music and break dancing. People will stop and listen because it's interesting. The message is being communicated in a form they can receive. A church with a vision of itself as a missionary church will incorporate a variety of forms in their own services as well. For the goal is not only to do things that make those already saved feel good but to expand the circle of the family of God.

Unfortunately, too many Christians are culturally paternalistic. They believe that their culture, their way of doing things, is right. The foreign mission field has seen too much of this paternalism, where the gospel is tied to Western social forms and values. For instance, the first thing women converts in the jungle do is put on blouses. The universal gospel is buried under secondary or even trivial issues. The problem of the Judaizers with whom the apostle Paul struggled is still present. As the early church saw growing numbers of Gentile converts, they had to decide, "Does a Gentile have to become a Jew before becoming a Christian?" The question of circumcism was not just a religious but also a cultural matter. The answer was no. Jews could remain Jews. Gentiles could remain Gentiles. But in Christ they transcended their difference to establish a unity that respected all persons for who they were. Fundamentalist churches that condemn drums and dancing reflect a paternalism that has no biblical basis but is rather a sign of cultural bias. One of my black friends accused fundamentalist whites of being uptight about their bodies in forbidding dancing. Such condemnation is patently absurd to someone raised in an Afro-American heritage. To be an effective missionary church, especially in the pluralistic culture of American cities, all forms of cultural paternalism must be dropped. We need to become multilingual in the forms we use to express our faith and love of God. We need to express the acceptance and flexibility of the first great missionary who said:

> For though I am free from all people, I have made myself a slave to all, that I might win the more. To the Jews I became as a Jew, in order to win Jews; to those under the law I became as one under the law—though not being myself under the law—that I might win those under the law. To those outside the law I became as one outside the law—not being without law toward God but under the law of Christ—that I might

win those outside the law. To the weak I became weak, that I might win the weak. I have become all things to all people, that I might by all means save some. I do it all for the sake of the gospel, that I may share in its blessings (1 Corinthians 9:19-23, adapted).

Any church that develops a missionary church mentality will pay a price. Missionaries always pay a price to fulfill their call. Cherished possessions, places, and people are left behind in response to the Lord's command to go. A church that catches the missionary vision will have to pay the price of setting aside concern for their own comfort, their favorite hymns, the coziness of a steady group of well-known friends. The church must take the risk of trusting the paradox of the gospel. Jesus said, "Whoever would save one's life will lose it; and whoever loses one's life for my sake and the gospel's will save it" (Mark 8:35, adapted). Churches bound by survival mentality strive to save their lives and hold onto what they value. But the result is that the churches will die and all will be lost anyway. How much better it is to lose it all by committing ourselves to Christ and the work of the gospel, to choose to give ourselves and our churches away. The paradox is that churches as well as individuals who sacrifice themselves, who serve others in love, will receive the rich fullness of God's blessings. As long as Dorchester Temple focused on itself, it shrank. Only when the people began to care about the issues of the neighborhood, when they began to share their faith with neighbors and friends, when they freed up their worship service to speak in forms outsiders could appreciate—only then did the church begin to flourish and grow. A church finds its life by giving it away.

The gospel paradox drives the people of a church back to the first element of the threefold journey, the vision of Christ present among us. Survival mentality doesn't see Jesus clearly, so the step of faith cannot be taken. Giving away the church resources in missions is a foolhardy risk of our rare commodities of people and money. But if church members have caught a vision of Christ, there is no way they can be content to stay in themselves. Jesus himself commands them to go out, and he gives the assurance that inspires the daring risk to be taken: "Lo, I am with you always, to the close of the age," (Matthew 28:20). In the presence of the risen Christ, we can know that no giving away of ourselves is a waste. Jesus said,

> "Truly, I say to you, there is no one who has left houses or brothers or sisters or mother or father or children or lands, for my sake and for the gospel, who will not receive a hundredfold now in this time, houses and brothers and sisters and mothers and children and lands, with persecutions, and in the age to come•eternal life" (Mark 10:29-30).

The blessings of God will come back to people and churches that are willing to sacrifice themselves for Christ's sake, even as Jesus says, "now in this time."

A Holistic Vision for Mission

A church can move out strongly on the journey of renewal with only a partial vision of mission, but a holistic vision will be the healthiest and clearest guide. The Bible presents three aspects of mission that lead directly into one another. To fragment the holistic scope of biblical mission is to fall short of what God requires of a church. A limited working out of vision is better than the stunted inwardness of survivalism, but hopefully it is just an intermediary stage on a journey to a more comprehensive understanding of Christ's call and the working out of that call in action.

A holistic vision of mission has three components: evangelism, meeting human need, and speaking prophetically. Each component relates to the other two, both in Scripture and in experience. A church that will break out of survival mentality would do well to examine forms of mission expressing each aspect of this holistic vision. The first component of a holistic vision of mission is evangelism, proclaiming the Good News of Jesus Christ and calling people to a vital relationship with him. Paul writes in Romans:

> For "Everyone who calls upon the name of the Lord will be saved."
> But how are people to call upon him in whom they have not believed? And how are they to believe in him of whom they have never heard? And how are they to hear without a preacher? And how can people preach unless they are sent? As it is written, "How beautiful are the feet of those who preach good news!" (Romans 10:13-15, adapted).

A church with a vision of itself as a missionary body will take seriously the task of evangelism. They will work at developing their witness in both organized and relational ways. All are responsible to be proclaimers of the Good News in some form. They will be reaching out to the unsaved and unchurched, seeking to bring them to faith and integrate them into the life of the congregation.

We did some programmatic evangelism. For one week each summer we would hold street meetings in playgrounds or on vacant lots within walking distance of the church. These meetings included live music, short films, evangelistic preaching, and members witnessing throughout the crowds that gathered. We held training sessions in personal witnessing prior to the meetings and conducted follow-up calls and visits. An occasional Bible study of four sessions was held to which neighbors interested in the Christian faith were invited.

These organized efforts had limited success. Some decisions for Christ were made, and a couple families came into the church. But the problems we encountered were similar to many churches with survival mentality backgrounds. We had an untrained laity, and I as pastor did not see evangelism as one of my strengths. We utilized the resources of a local urban ministries center, but our program never became a high-powered success. Still, we did benefit from additional visibility in our community and growth among the members in sharing their faith. A vacation Bible school program, which demanded more energy from the members, produced better results. We were flooded with children and youth. Some became regular participants in our church programs, and we began seeing some new parents at the services. A deliberate outreach effort was made toward parents through a parents' night and an ice-cream social.

The most significant evangelistic impact was made through the network of friends and relatives of our members. As the church began to gather momentum in renewal, people got excited about what was happening and invited those close to them. A chart could be drawn up showing the growing connections, a church "family tree." One woman came to check out the "moral education" her children were getting in the Sunday school. She was moved by what she heard and made a commitment to Christ. Her children brought friends; she brought a friend. Her friend became a Christian, brought her whole family, and on it went. This process of relationship evangelism was replicated throughout the church.

The key to the success of this form of evangelism was that the life and message of the church was attractive. Christ was presented clearly in the sermons. I deliberately avoided theological jargon and fancy words that would exclude many listeners; profound thoughts can be communicated in plain language. The music was in cultural forms that people could readily identify. The prayers by the congregation and the pastor expressed basic feelings and concerns in everyday language. When visitors came, whether invited by friends or simply dropped in on their own, they found a church that was accessible to them. They left with a good feeling about what was happening there. One family who joined the church was referred to us by a one-time visitor!

Visitors needed follow-up in order to be reached consistently. Pastoral visits during the following week were a high priority in my work. Many who joined spoke about the significance of such visits to them. But to stay in a church, most newcomers need to establish a small network of new relationships quickly. Opportunities for relationship building need to be developed. Some members organized an after-service coffee hour both to facilitate relationship building within our diverse membership and to allow newcomers an easy setting for meeting folks. Evangelistic harvests don't happen automatically; they must be cultivated by the whole congregation.

As people in the congregation move out to take the Good News of Christ to their neighbors, they will discover much deep and profound human need. Proclaiming the love of God in evangelism puts us in contact with people in pain who need that love expressed in very concrete and practical forms. As the apostle John exhorts, "But if any one has the world's goods and sees one's brothers or sisters in need, yet closes one's heart against them, how does God's love abide in that person? Little children, let us not love in word or speech but in deed and in truth" (1 John 3:17-18, adapted). Mission, then, must include meeting human need, fleshing out the love of Christ in actions.

Human need can and must be addressed in two different ways: mercy and justice. The prophet Micah proclaimed: "What does the LORD require of you? To act justly and to love mercy and to walk humbly with your God" (Micah 6:8, NIV). Mercy is the immediate response to human need: feeding the hungry, clothing the naked, sheltering the homeless. Such acts and ministries of compassion will always be needed in this sinful world, and our faith will compel us to do acts of mercy.

Our vacation Bible school included breakfast and lunch for the children. Our superintendent noticed that some children were eating more ravenously than mere growing children. She discovered that they were hungry; one girl even showed the lethargy of serious malnutrition. Out of mercy we expanded our feeding program to breakfasts at Sunday church school and lunches during some of our other summer youth activities. Groceries were sent to the families from our small food pantry. Mercy required that plain bread be served to these children alongside the Bread of Life.

But mercy is not enough; we are commanded to "seek justice, correct oppression; defend the orphan, plead for the widow" (Isaiah 1:17, adapted). A church with a vision for mission that is reaching out evangelistically with any degree of sensitivity and wisdom will encounter the social structures, dynamics, and relationships that crush people. The problems of racism, unemployment, poor education, poverty, and shattered families all have bearing on the well-being of the individuals we reach for Christ.

In the city of Boston a housing crisis is sweeping the poor away, leaving many people in our churches and those who receive our Good News in desperate straits. Emergency shelters are needed but do little for helping put the pieces back together. Mercy helps in a crisis, but justice is necessary to open up the possibility for abundant life. People have to have homes, places that are decent for life and growth. So in this case, justice means working to insure that people can obtain affordable housing that they can control or at least be secure in. The church established a housing committee to explore ways to address this crisis and empower the members of our congregation and others in the neighborhood who were most vulnerable in the housing crisis. The risk of failure in such a venture is high, for seeking justice puts us in touch with some of the thorniest and most perennial problems facing society. However, serious discipleship and a compelling vision for mission will bring us to the point of rolling up our sleeves to tackle the most difficult issues around us.

Working for justice quickly leads to the third component of a vision for mission—speaking prophetically to our generation. The evils that crush people are seen and need to be addressed by the Word of God. Institutional evils such as the escalation of military expenditures at the cost of cutbacks on human services need to be held up to the light of Scripture, both in churches and in our messages to society at large. Individual evils such as the sexual permissiveness and materialism that characterize this generation need to be confronted directly. Sin is present personally and socially, and as the church moves out in mission, the raw, ugly damage of sin is starkly evident. As Jesus denounced the Pharisees for devouring widows' homes (Mark 12:40), the church that goes into the world as he did needs to speak the prophetic word courageously to its contemporary generation.

Prophetic witness can take place from the pulpit. Though most of my sermons were directed toward shaping the life of discipleship and the community of the church, occasionally a national or global issue cried out for a clear biblical challenge. Preaching on contemporary issues is a vital part of setting forth "the whole counsel of God." Martin Luther said, "If you preach the gospel in all aspects with the exception of the issues which deal specifically with your time, you are not preaching the gospel at all."[1] A pastor owes it to God and to the congregation to translate faithfully the prophetic message into contemporary contexts.

If the church as a whole catches the vision for prophetic witness, ministries can be established to reach out beyond the walls of the sanctuary. At Dorchester Temple we developed a peacemakers' group that worked on issues of nuclear war and United States policy in Central America. Any effort to witness prophetically is bound to raise controversy, and this was experienced in our church as well. We found that if the social activists extended themselves in other areas of the church life, i.e., came out for cleanup days, helped put on mission suppers, or taught in the Sunday school, the

---

[1]Quoted in Ronald J. Sider, *Rich Christians in an Age of Hunger: A Biblical Study* (Downers Grove, Ill.: Inter-Varsity Press, 1977), page 58.

broader membership had more trust in the Christian integrity of the activists even if they disagreed with their politics. Mutual respect and extending the freedom to speak and act out of one's conscience were nurtured and encouraged as we challenged one another to apply the gospel to the issues we faced in our city and nation.

The Great Commission as recorded in Luke's Gospel brings mission full circle. Jesus said that "repentance and forgiveness of sins should be preached in his name to all nations" (Luke 24:48). Prophetic witness pinpoints the personal and social sins that require repentance, and evangelism points people to the provision of God's grace and forgiveness in transforming power.

A church with a renewed vision for mission will go into the world as Christ's ambassadors to carry on his work. Instead of being the worthless, insipid salt of survivalism, the mission-minded congregation will be genuinely salty, bringing salvation, healing, and liberation to humanity and glory to God.

The Vision Bearer: The Person

F or the vision of God, the church, and mission to become a dynamic, energizing guide into renewal, there must be a person who lifts up the vision. Just as the prophet Ezekiel stood over the valley of dry bones and proclaimed the word of the Lord, a person must be raised up to fill the role of vision bearer. The vision bearer proclaims God's word to the dying church, and as the Spirit moves, the new work of God takes hold. A mighty army is raised up where before there were only scattered remains.

The vision bearer plays a key role in the process of renewal. This is a particular aspect of ministry that is often neglected, for the focus tends to be on preaching, teaching, administrative, and pastoral skills. These are fundamentally important gifts for pastoral leadership, but the gift of being a vision bearer is essential for renewal to take place. In this chapter the nature of the vision bearer as a person will be set forth. In the following chapter the work of the vision bearer will be spelled out.

Who the Vision Bearer Is

The vision bearer is usually the pastor of the church. Because of the time involved in a pastor's work, the opportunity to address the congregation every week, and the connection with each member of the congregation, the pastor is the person in the most pivotal position in a church's life. For better or worse, the pastor has the greatest potential for influencing individuals and the group psyche of the entire congregation. Many churches have a strong sense of vision, so their pastors perhaps need not be adequate vision bearers. But as survivalist churches are experiencing a famine of vision, it is utterly critical for the pastor to be a visionary person. When there is a pastoral change, this should be one of the key considerations for whoever plays a part in the decision-making process, from the local level to denominational staff.

A pastor without vision who has succumbed to survival mentality is in no position to lead the people of God out of their valley of dry bones. I've seen churches in a tailspin as the pastors stagger on in a fog of depression and despair. A pastor's discouragement reflects the survivalist thinking of the congregation, and instead of countering it, he or she gives in to it, creating a negative resonance. The decline accelerates in a vicious downward cycle. Whatever the reason that a pastor stays in such a bad situation, the church will suffer.

But even a more benign pastoral leader doesn't help. Someone who just loves the folks may make wonderful friends but won't be able to rebuild the church. Pastors may assume the role of chaplain on the *Titanic;* they comfort the folks as the ship goes down, a role that may be necessary. Too often, however, their comforting ministry starts before the ship is awash. There is still time to avoid disaster, still time to mend leaks, still time to chart a new course, even if at a slow speed. We should not give up on our churches too early, for remember who our God is. God is the one who raises up a mighty army from dry bones and already has a remnant present even in the survivalist churches.

The pastor, then, is the pivotal inspirational figure. A visionary pastor can attract the remnant people in the congregation who are willing to give of themselves to enable the church to see a new day. A visionary pastor can attract newcomers who want to join with a going concern. A visionary pastor will be used by God to gather a core of visionary people who will become the yeast in the rest of the congregation, helping the whole batch to rise.

However, for many survivalist churches there is a leadership void when it comes to vision. The pastor for whatever reason is not a vision bearer. This presents a handicap to the renewal process, but not an insurmountable one. There can be vision bearers among the women and men of the congregation who serve as more than just a remnant. These laypersons are filled with the type of vision spelled out earlier, and they aren't waiting for something to happen somehow someday. They take on the work of the vision bearer in their more limited circles. This can be very threatening to a discouraged pastor. He or she can feel like King Saul did about David: "They have ascribed to David ten thousands, and to me they have ascribed thousands; and what more can he have but the kingdom?" (1 Samuel 18:8). It is difficult for the pastor to accept and support the ministry and zeal of such a person, but one must do so and even be personally open to be touched by the vision of this member of the flock. It takes a measure of humility to admit to a need of this nature, and if the pastor can do it, then a significant step on the road to personal and church renewal will be taken.

It is also difficult to be a vision bearer who is not a pastor. The lack of pastoral leadership and support can lead to discouragement, judgmentalism, and eventual withdrawal from the life of that church. It takes grace and endurance to stay in such a church and maintain the vision amid such a sterile environment, but in due time God will honor this kind of commitment.

A Passionate Matter

The vision of the pastor must be a passionate matter. It must be held with a faith and hope that go to the root of one's being. Many people obtain seminary education, and many can learn to do exegesis. Speaking skills can be refined and administrative techniques mastered. But no formal education can teach a heart to have vision. Vision is caught not taught. It is a gift of God, not a programmed result from a seminary or conference. It is a call from God felt in one's bones, and it is utterly essential to fulfill the role of vision bearer.

Why must the vision be a passionate matter for the vision bearer? Because it will be put to a strenuous test. Survivalist churches are so filled with problems that they will overwhelm those who come just to do a good job. Their stressful challenges will even beat down many hopeful and passionately dedicated leaders. To weather the storms, the call must be present deep within, guiding, urging, sustaining over the long haul. Jeremiah had a difficult unappreciated ministry. The nation of Judah refused to respond to the vision he proclaimed, so he felt like giving up, packing it in. In Jeremiah 20 he shares his struggle, and the call surfaces as an inescapable part of his very being: "There is in my heart as it were a burning fire shut up in my bones, and I am weary with holding it in, and I cannot" (Jeremiah 20:9). The vision and call are integral to one's personhood.

Urban churches especially need pastoral leadership committed to Christian witness in the context of the city. Too many urban churches have been stepping-stones for career advancement. They are the only available openings, so new seminary graduates take them until they can get a "good" church in the suburbs. Sometimes this abuse of urban pastorates is supported by denominational executives who steer the inexperienced seminary graduates into the most difficult and decaying churches. The new pastor becomes cannon fodder, a raw recruit pushed to the front to be chewed up by the big guns of survival mentality. City churches need to have leaders who are committed to urban ministry, vision bearers whose call includes being called specifically to the city, pastors who are there because they want to be. Cannon fodder and ladder climbers will not help.

The people of the congregation can tell if their pastor really believes what is preached. They know if their setting is embraced as God's opportunity or is regarded as an unfortunate necessity. When the pastor really believes and lives out the vision, then the people will be more eager to follow. They will give their trust because they know their leader cares for them and their place in the world.

Rooted in God

A pastor can hold a sound vision very passionately in his or her heart and yet get into serious personal trouble. I know, for that is what happened to me. When I came to Dorchester Temple, I was filled with ideas, youthful zeal, boundless energy, and a vision I was eager to proclaim. I worked hard for thirteen months in the church and in the community. Then I had a physical breakdown. A normal hay fever allergy put me out of commission for two months. I had worked myself physically and spiritually to exhaustion. I was burned-out.

Behind my burn-out was a messianic complex, a mental state to which pastors and vision bearers are very susceptible. I was going to save Dorchester Temple. I was going to save Codman Square, our decaying neighborhood. I seemed competent in so many areas—a gifted, talented person. My vision was very good and biblical. But my faith was actually in myself, though I didn't recognize it at the time. I was trusting in my knowledge, my preaching skill, and my energy level to turn the tide. I was the messiah in my own mind, but I discovered that I was utterly inadequate for the task.

The job of Messiah had already been taken. It did not fall to Dan Buttry or anybody else to save Dorchester Temple; that was Christ's task. As I meditated upon my breakdown, I realized I was not responsible for the church. I was responsible for myself and the stewardship of my gifts. I was responsible for following God's direction as best I could discern it. But the responsibility for the church lies upon Christ. His shoulders alone are sufficient to carry that burden.

As a pastor and vision bearer, I discovered a profound need to be rooted in God. Of course, we always speak of being dependent upon God; we're supposed to say that. But to live what we preach and integrate such dependence into our daily mental and emotional pattern is a personal journey with no shortcuts. Jesus had already told us this was the case: "I am the vine, and you are the branches. Whoever remains in me, and I in him, will bear much fruit; for you can do nothing without me" (John 15:5, TEV). I had preached on this text before, led Bible studies upon it, but had to learn personally how to abide in a new way, a deeper way.

Not only was I hurting myself by my self-sufficiency, I was also hurting the church I pastored. They needed vision, a vision I was preaching. But it had to be rooted in God for them, so how could I lead them into the elementary steps of renewal when I was not practicing the upward journey myself? I was living in contradiction to what I was preaching; as a result I was bound to burn out even as the church had burned out over the past decades. I had to humble myself before God, repent of my self-sufficiency, and allow God's Spirit free reign in myself before I could faithfully fulfill my role as vision bearer.

The result of living in this fashion was very liberating to me. I was more relaxed about what I did, about what was accomplished and what wasn't achieved. I worked just as diligently but with a freer spirit. And in the months that followed, the spirit of renewal began to flow across our congregation.

Perhaps one of the problems with pastoral leadership is our models for ministry. I was pastoring along the lines of the prophets of Baal who were challenged by Elijah at Mount Carmel. They worked and danced feverishly to try to get the fire started. They cajoled and pleaded with their god, but nothing happened. They finally collapsed, exhausted by the effort, even as I did. Pastors who hold up seventy- to eighty-hour work weeks as the ideal are probably operating by the prophet-of-Baal ministry model. They see themselves as indispensable to God's work. They believe that if they don't run themselves ragged, the church will fall apart. This is a sign of a messianic complex, and we as vision bearers must turn aside from the spirit and style of such self-centered messianism. Its very essence is contrary to the Christ-centered faith necessary for renewal.

In stark contrast stands the ministry model of Elijah. He is calm, deliberate, and careful in his work. He builds the altar, lays the fire, sets out the sacrifice. He preaches to the people and prays to God. There is a quiet assurance in his actions, a steadiness in his pace, and a confidence in his faith. Elijah is depending upon God to play the key role. Then fire falls from heaven and consumes the sacrifice and the altar.

The work of renewal is God's work, not the vision bearer's. The vision bearer, like Elijah, can labor carefully to prepare for the renewal, but only God sends the fire from heaven. A pastor rooted in God will have the quiet trust to wait upon the moving of the Spirit. After all, the vision lifted up before the people is that God is powerfully present among God's people today, so the pastoral ministry needs to be existentially dependent upon God to fulfill that role. If God had not answered Elijah's prayer on Mount Carmel, Elijah would have been a dead fool, but he didn't even contemplate that possibility. He knew God's faithfulness and cast his own fate upon it. God does not let down the vision bearers.

The Vision Bearer: The Work

*T*he vision bearer's task has four elements. The first element is simply loving the people. The next two elements involve lifting up the vision for the congregation to see. Preaching and teaching communicate the vision by word, and modeling communicates the vision by example. The fourth element of this work is interpretation. As the vision unfolds in the life of the church and as their journey progresses, there is a need to interpret the shared experience of the congregation.

Loving

The first component of the vision bearer's work is loving. The Apostle Paul tells us, ". . . If I have all faith, so as to remove mountains, but have not love, I am nothing" (1 Corinthians 13:2). Visionaries who can see the problems and see the way to whip the church into shape but fail to love the folks will also fail in leading the church out of survival mentality. In other contexts vision bearers need not be lovers of people, but survivalist churches are wounded and full of broken, discouraged members. They need love expressed in grace and acceptance. The vision bearer must love with the gentle determination seen in the suffering servant in Isaiah's prophesy: ". . . A bruised reed he will not break, and a dimly burning wick he will not quench . . ." (Isaiah 42:3). A vision bearer needs first to be a good pastor.

Too many times pastors come into survivalist churches full of vision and short on love. They may see their work as "prophetic," needing to shake up the people and get things rolling again. Without love, the result is bound to be frustration for the pastor and resentment among the congregation. The pastor will eventually leave, and the church will not be better off. In fact, the situation may be worse, for their defenses against change will have been entrenched a little deeper. We may have the faith to move the mountains of spiritual decline and deadness, but without love we will be nothing.

Love, for the vision bearer, is not holding people's hands as the *Titanic* settles in the water. Love desires the fullness of Christ for people. It is a caring for individuals that longs to see them each attain the abundant life of Christ in their own particular life setting. Survival mentality is nowhere near abundant life, so love will not be content to console the mourners at the funeral of the body of Christ.

Instead, love brings the vision, but in gentleness and patience. The vision is softly blown into people's hearts like the gentle blowing on the faint embers of a dying fire. Impatient and harsh blowing just stirs up the ash, makes a mess, and hastens the final extinguishing of the fire. But the soft, persistent effort will lead to a flame finally springing forth ready to ignite new fuel. Such is the labor of love in the ministry of vision bearing. Time needs to be spent with people, caring, listening, hearing their fears and dreams, and with gentle persistence lifting up the light of hope.

As people know they are loved, they will place their trust in the leadership of the vision bearer. Trust is not automatically given to anyone, especially not to pastors coming in to lead battered and worried survivalist churches. Trust must be earned. But once people place their trust in a leader, they are willing to take risks and break new ground. I spent the entire first year of my pastorate concentrating on visiting folks and getting to know them in their own context. As I built upon that foundation of caring relationships, I found the trust the members placed in me growing. I found I could "get away with things" more—introduce a change in the worship service, begin a new ministry, get more involved in the community. People would let me lead them into new areas because they trusted me. Once they invested themselves and their scarce resources, I wasn't going to drop them and head out to the suburbs for a bigger, wealthier church. They knew they were loved, so they began to trust me and the work of vision bearing.

Preaching and Teaching

The tasks of preaching and teaching are central to the ministry of any pastor. Everything from evangelism to personal discipleship to social ethics to basic biblical knowledge is covered by the preaching and teaching ministry. The vision is also part of the content to be covered. In fact, there is no more central place in which vision is communicated than the Sunday sermon. In the worship service, the whole church is gathered together. Other settings are important for growth and development of vision, but in the worship service the Spirit of God can move upon the whole people. Since renewal of the group vision is the key to church renewal, the sermon is a central element of the vision bearer's work if the vision bearer is a pastor.

Through the sermon and through Bible studies and adult classes, the content of the vision can be expressed. Each of the dimensions of the threefold journey can be explored in-depth. If the overall vision is clearly and repeatedly stated, people can study the component parts in detail without losing sight of the forest or the trees. In renewal, the forest is essential to comprehend. Many survivalist churches have people with very well-developed understanding of the details, the trees. But they have lost sight of the larger picture; their vision is stunted. So through teaching and preaching, the vision bearer can help people grasp the whole of God's call for the church.

Besides the content of the vision, the preaching and teaching ministry can be a great vehicle for lifting up the spirit of the vision as well. The proclaimer of the word must communicate the passion of faith and hope or else the vision will come forth stillborn. It must be alive in the heart of the preacher as mentioned earlier, and the proclamation needs to be infused with this aliveness from one's inner being. Vision is not just an academic model or a shared set of understood beliefs. It is a living faith, a living hope. These intangible but very real and very recognizable qualities are just as important as the content of the preached word.

The Bible is full of illustrations of vision, both in content and in spirit, which can be turned into relevant sermons. The prophet Haggai faced a situation of decline that is uncomfortably familiar to survivalist churches. The temple had been destroyed, and later the returning exiles tried to rebuild upon the old ruins. But their condition was rather pitiful compared to the greatness of "the good old days." Haggai spoke, " 'Who is left among you that saw this house in its former glory? How do you see it now? Is it not in your sight as nothing?' " (Haggai 2:3). Israel's older folks were hung up by their memories; they could only remember what was no longer and would never be again, just as the church members bogged down in survival mentality. But the prophet's message from the Lord is full of visionary hope and inspiration: " 'Take courage . . . work, for I am with you . . . my Spirit abides among you; fear not . . . I will fill this house with splendor . . . in this place I will give prosperity, says the LORD of hosts' " (Haggai 2:4-9). What a message for despairing people! I preached Haggai's message from the Lord shortly after I'd arrived at Dorchester Temple. The vision of God's presence as a source of power to labor joyfully in the present was as needed by us as by Israel in Haggai's day.

Joshua and Caleb inspired another visionary sermon. The

timid spirit of survivalist churches is akin to the nay saying of the spies Moses sent out. Ten of the spies were intimidated by the giants and fortresses at Canaan. They said, ". . . We seemed to ourselves like grasshoppers . . ." (Numbers 13:33). The problems of changing neighborhoods, shrinking and aging memberships, decaying buildings, and chronic financial distress make a congregation feel like grasshoppers, defeated nobodies. Joshua and Caleb saw the same problems as the other spies, but they also had a strong vision of who their God was. They proclaimed, ". . . The LORD is with us; do not fear them [the Canaanites or problems]" (Numbers 14:9). Joshua and Caleb were almost stoned for their visionary appeal, a fate not too far from what some pastors experience! It may be that the contemporary church will hear the call of faith and not go back to the wilderness but rather press on toward the land of promise.

The Bible has a rich mine of material to use in lifting up the vision of God's presence and the divine call to journey in faith. Sermons can be preached from passages such as Joel 2:28-29; Joshua 1:1-11; 2 Timothy 1:7; Hebrews 12:1-2; Philippians 3:4-16, to name a few. The story of Nehemiah makes for a great series on rebuilding with divinely inspired vision. The preacher and teacher needs to set forth these messages of Scripture again and again, for they are the most pertinent to the church at this point in its life. By putting forth the vision in its vast biblical richness, the vision bearer is readying the altar and sacrifice of the church so the fire can fall from heaven. The preacher needs to be patient, remembering that only God can light the fire. The preacher also needs to be persistent, speaking the message repeatedly in a variety of forms so that the people will be readied for the movement of God's renewing.

The Modeling Ministry

The vision proclaimed in the preaching and teaching ministry must also be demonstrated. The vision bearer needs to model in his or her own life the vision lifted up in one's words. Living out the vision in one's life is critical for it to catch hold in the life of the congregation. Someone has to show the way it all works, and who better than the one preaching about it?

Modeling the vision is a humbling and challenging task. None of us can hope to incarnate fully God's call in our lives, but we can hope and expect our lives to demonstrate God's working so that others will be able to see. The apostle Paul did not shy away from putting his own life before the people as a model to follow. "I urge you, then, be imitators of me," he instructed the members of the Corinthian church (1 Corinthians 4:16). Further on in the same letter he pointed them beyond himself: "Be imitators of me as I am of Christ" (1 Corinthians 11:1). The vision of Christian discipleship is not an abstraction but is fleshed out before their eyes in Paul himself.

Putting oneself in the spotlight can become a powerful temptation. Pride can creep in. The dream of the personality cult can lurk subtly around the edges of the vision. But Paul's modeling had an antidote to the poison of pride. He modeled his weaknesses, failures, and struggles as well as his faithfulness. He told his apprentice, Timothy, "I am the foremost of sinners; but I received mercy for this reason, that in me, as the foremost, Jesus Christ might display his perfect patience for an example to those who were to believe in him for eternal life" (1 Timothy 1:15-16). An appropriate modeling of discipleship involves transparency regarding our places of brokenness so that people can see the working of Christ's gracious power. The vision bearer needs to model confession as well as commitment. I mentioned earlier a Sunday when I confessed some specific sins to the congregation and asked for their forgiveness. A year later our youth group was responsible for the morning worship service. The theme they chose was leadership. One of the young men spoke about humility and confession, relating the impact of my earlier confession on his developing image of Christian discipleship and leadership. The vision bearer was being watched with impressionable eyes. Our modeling is a serious responsibility.

In survivalist churches modeling needs to focus on the points where survivalism is choking out the spiritual vitality and hope of the church. The visionary outlook must be applied to the weekly and monthly issues that confront the congregation—what to do about the old furnace, the leaky roof, the death of a big giver, the move of a key worker. Reflexive responses coming out of survival mentality need to be countered by an alternative approach to the problems. The vision bearer can take advantage of the occasions of crisis to demonstrate the new way of looking at situations. He or she could suggest that instead of haranguing people about church bills and manipulating their guilt, perhaps a new tactic could be tried. The vision of renewal in worship, personal and communal growth, and outreach could be lifted up. Stewardship presents an opportunity to aid the work of renewal. We give, not to avoid default, but to enable ministry. At first people may not respond positively; but with patience, love, and long-suffering, the vision bearer's message does begin to break through.

The vision bearer needs to model the vision of God as present. In the last chapter the need was set forth for the vision bearer to be rooted deeply in God. The hidden life of the leader should be one of a growing relationship with the living God. But to communicate the reality of that hidden dependence, the vision bearer needs to express that faith and confidence in group settings with others in church, at board and committee meetings, in home visits, as well as the corporate worship. The vision bearer should take the lead by demonstrating faith-filled prayer and decision making that is open to the moving and guidance of the Spirit. People will tend to operate in familiar patterns, which in survival mentality are often limiting or even self-defeating. An alternative mentality and an alternative way of approaching problems and decisions needs to be lived in front of the folks. Then they can see that new paths can be taken and can even work.

The vision bearer also models the vision of the church by exhibiting a reconciling spirit, reaching out to all people. The vision bearer should take the lead in extending the arms of welcome to all who come, especially newcomers that are a threat to the homogeneity of the congregation. The value of each person as a member of the body needs to be affirmed from the pulpit and also by the words of praise and encouragement given directly to individuals.

The work of spiritual nurture that the church undertakes is modeled not just in being a teacher but in showing oneself as a learner too. Vision bearers are disciples, pupils who are keenly aware of their need to be taught by the Master. So we can testify to our own journey, be transparent about the processes of Christ working within us. If people can see the openness and the normalness of the quest for spiritual maturity, they can be freed from the games and isolation that occur so much in survivalist churches. When we all understand that it is okay to be in process, then we can be free to be honest. We can get to know one another and build bonds of trust and respect because we don't need to hide behind masks of self-sufficiency. Since the pastor is often put on a pedestal, when he or she models the growing process with its acknowledged incompleteness and hunger to be more like Christ, then others can take the risk of being real, too. As more people become honest about their lives and journey, a community of growing people emerges: the church living out the vision of spiritual nurture.

I experienced this dynamic of personal vulnerability leading to deeper community in the church as a whole when I preached out of a major struggle in my own family. My wife, Sharon, and I had been torn by the pain of infertility and unsuccessful medical treatment for six years. After I shared the deep struggle we experienced and the growth and healing that came to us through God's grace, many people came up to me after the service, or in the days that followed, exposing their own raw places and wounds. Some of these revelations came from friends I thought I had known well, but only taking a risk to share myself made them feel safe enough and accepted enough to share their deepest sorrows. Out of that mutual sharing came a more profound sense of the church as a community of sinners and wounded people bathed in the healing grace of Christ.

With survivalist churches so desperately needy, the strong pull of inwardness needs to be countered by modeling mission to the world. Sometimes the mission emphasis will focus on the foreign fields, but in urban churches especially there is a multitude of mission needs and opportunities right in the neighborhood. Though the church may not have energy or interest to tackle any of the pressing problems in the community, the vision bearer can model the vision of God's future for the church by getting involved in at least one ministry reaching beyond the congregation. Perhaps nobody from the church will be interested or even supportive, but the vision bearer should at least start. One pastor I know gave a tithe of his pastoral time to community concerns. My wife and I became involved in forming a community development corporation for our neighborhood. The people who are responding to the vision will begin to join in the work and will come up with ideas of their own. As the pastor demonstrates a concern for mission, those who may have not seen their church as an effective channel for outreach to the neighborhood are encouraged and begin to take the risks of starting up new ministries. One stagnating church in Boston got a new clergy couple who were filled with vision for the church and the community. They became the catalysts that prompted some members to start a food pantry ministry that now involves the efforts of a number of members.

The impact of modeling mission on the church's mentality is twofold. The members begin moving beyond themselves into a concern for the world. In service they grow spiritually as they learn more about compassion, practical love, and as they have to go back to the Lord who is their source for strength and their fount of love. At this point the vision is catching hold, the flame is licking the altar.

The Ministry of Interpretation

One summer my wife and I took a vacation through the maritime provinces of Canada. We toured many of the historical sites: the old forts, the partially restored town of Louisburg, and the local museums. We were impressed with the guides whom we met at almost every stop. They filled us in on the history in such a way that these unfamiliar places and times with their issues and politics became alive. The work of these guides enriched our travels. We had never been in this area before, yet, thanks to their interpretative comments, we could more knowledgeably take in the sights. Such is the ministry of interpretation by the vision bearer. The congregation, and probably the vision bearer as well, has never been in this setting before. As their journey unfolds, the members are faced with new issues and dynamics, with stages of congregational life they may not recognize or understand. The vision bearer can interpret the experiences the whole group is going through to place them in the larger context of the progressive journey toward God. This is especially true once the congregation has begun to break out of survival mentality. Although there is excitement at the winds of renewal blowing in the church, there can also be confusion in the face of new issues and lingering fears and doubts from old mental and spiritual habits. The ministry of interpretation helps people see how the vision is developing in their particular present moment so people can be encouraged and strengthened.

In Dorchester Temple after our "breakout" service of January 1980, we went through a couple years of high energy and vitality. Many new members came into the church, and a lot of creative changes took place. Then many folks began to feel frustrated and started picking at one another. People loved the church and yet were growing uneasy. Some were acting out their uneasiness by complaining and arguing. Finally, one woman gave me an extensive, thoughtful statement of her feelings and where they seemed to be coming from. All of a sudden it hit me—we were in an identity crisis. The old Dorchester Temple with its definition of who we were and how we operated had passed away. But what was growing in its place, while dynamically alive, was still undefined and unsure of itself. We were a church going through adolescence. We needed to come to an understanding of who we were that was clearly delineated and that incorporated the new vision dawning among us.

The following Sunday I preached on this topic, laying out that I saw us in an identity crisis, what the issues were, and how we could go about resolving them. The response was like having a light turned on in a dark room. The affirmation came back, "Yes, that's what we've been feeling." Now, that the church recognized were it was, we could begin working together to resolve the issues.

The deacons began a process of interviewing the entire group of people active in the church to find out their perspectives and experiences. Each deacon was given a diverse cross section of the church in order to encounter directly some of the breadth of who we had become. The deacons then pulled together a report that set forth who we were with our strengths and weaknesses, exploring our diversity and direction. The report was presented to the congregation, which then interacted about it in a long but stimulating business meeting. Through this process we got a fairly solid idea of who we had become.

The next step was to determine where we were going. The deacons drafted a new covenant for the church that reflected the vision of the threefold journey. The executive board worked on a structural overhaul to bring our organizational processes in line with that vision. When both the new covenant and the bylaws had been accepted, the identity of the "new" Dorchester Temple had been expressed and affirmed in a number of forms. Many people, especially the leaders, had shared in the journey of self-discovery. Because of my ministry of interpretation in sermons and in the board meetings, people were kept abreast of the process. Periodically there were opportunities for expression of each individual's sense of who we were and where we were, through being interviewed by the deacons, participating in small discussion groups at the business meetings, and voicing concerns and insights to the larger group of members. The high frustration level dissipated as people understood what our growth issue was and recognized we were doing something about it.

The ministry of interpretation touches many of the pastoral roles and tasks. Preaching can be a time for speaking directly to the particular stages of the congregation's journey, identifying where the congregation is, what the issues are, and some biblical perspectives to shed light on our journey. Psalm 119:105 says, "Thy word is a lamp to my feet and a light to my path." The interpreter shines the beam of the Word onto the path being traveled. For example, during our "identity crisis" I spoke from the pulpit about what was happening, then turned to the biblical teaching of the church to lift up guidelines to help shape our new sense of identity and purpose. Such preaching is timely and relevant to the needs of the moment, yet provides the directional beacon of God's abiding Word.

There are other moments for the exercise of the ministry of interpretation. Committee and board meetings are great forums for having deeper discussions of what is happening and forging a consensus about what the issues are and how to address them. The temptation is to get lost in the details of agenda items and the urgent crisis demanding attention (i.e., the furnace breaking down) and neglect the overall context, the big picture, which gives meaning to the particular issues. The vision bearer has an opportunity to raise the larger questions of direction, purpose, and goals in these smaller group settings. Leadership retreats or occasional weekend sessions can provide opportunities for boards or committees to step back from agenda items and analyze and address the deeper concerns. When the discussion focuses on goals, tension may develop between "the glass is half full" mind-set and "the glass is half empty" mind-set, those who think everything is fine and those who think things are going poorly. The ministry of interpretation can be used to clarify and celebrate the water that is in the cup. Specifically note areas of progress and strength. After all, half full is further along than empty! But the interpreter moves on to show the challenge left in the half empty glass. New goals can be set to move the church further along on its journey. We never arrive, but are called to press on to fill more of the cup of God's blessing.

Pastoral conversations with individuals can be an excellent opportunity for interpretation. Everybody has a perspective on the church's life, and every perspective is uniquely colored by the experiences of the individual. Personal experiences, dreams, and frustrations can be set within the larger framework of what God is doing in the whole body. Few people can touch the diversity of a local church like the pastor. So the pastor can share the sense of the growing edge of the church at the present moment with the individual members.

The ministry of interpretation is a key component of the work of the vision bearer. Through the exercise of this ministry, the congregation is kept on track in its journey following the Lord's vision. Though none of us has ever been this way before, the interpreter can pick up the dynamics and growing edges of the moment and lift them out of the particular events and issues in which they are incarnated. Then the whole congregation can deal more intelligently and strongly with the challenges set before them as they journey on in discipleship.

Barriers to Renewal: Old Wineskins

O n the journey of renewal the pilgrim church encounters many barriers, obstacles that block progress and even threaten to end the journey altogether. The rebirth of vision in a church can go a long way to overcoming these barriers, but each of them also needs direct, specific attention if it is to be dealt with effectively. In the face of such challenges, the church will need leadership with pastoral spirit and style matched with technical skills in organizational management.

The barriers dealt with may relate to forms or to people. Some barriers are "old wineskins" of tradition and organizational structure. Other barriers are in the human heart, from "the flesh." The old attitudes that can fester in a congregation and stifle the work of God will be dealt with in the next chapter. This chapter will cover the organizational booby traps that may need to be defused for safe passage through the renewal process.

Tradition

A survivalist church is a church with a long history. Many traditions have developed over the decades. These traditions usually grew out of a dynamic vision that inspired the members and crystalized parts of the Christian experience for them. But as a new generation grows up, as newcomers enter the church from vastly different backgrounds, as the surrounding community changes, the traditions can fade in significance to all but the survivalists. A gulf can develop between the traditions, which do not speak to the newcomers, and the experience of new vision and new life, which has to find its own expressions, rituals, and forms. New traditions are needed, but the old traditions still dominate, for they are maintained by the people still controlling the decision-making process in the church.

Jesus encountered the clash of tradition and new life in his ministry. As he came, announcing the Good News of the kingdom of God, he was attacked by the Pharisees, the keepers of the old ways. When questioned about the traditional practices of fasting, Jesus told two parables:

> "No one sews a piece of unshrunk cloth on an old garment; if he does, the patch tears away from it, the new from the old, and a worse tear is made. And no one puts new wine into old wineskins; if he does, the wine will burst the skins, and the wine is lost, and so are the skins; but new wine is for fresh skins" (Mark 2:21-22).

Change comes with the ferment of the new wine; it needs room to expand, flexibility, openness. If traditions are like an old wineskin, hard and unmoving, then trouble is brewing. The new wine of change will burst the skins and be spilled. Translated into a survivalist church, that means conflict will erupt which will weaken the already declining church, and the new wine of people with vision will give up and go elsewhere.

But traditions aren't bad. When he was criticized by the Pharisees about what his disciples did on the sabbath, Jesus replied: "The sabbath was made for people, not people for the Sabbath; so the Son of man is lord even of the sabbath" (Mark 2:27-28, adapted). Traditions are created to serve us in relating to God, forming community, or expressing our witness. Traditions are means not ends, servants not masters. Jesus is the only Lord, and he is Lord of all the traditions of the church, so we need to develop his perspective about our traditions. Are they fostering our growth as people and as a congregation? Are they opening up new perspectives, revealing greater depths of meaning to us, creating new dimensions to our vision? Or have they become a form that has lost touch with the reality once expressed? Jesus rebuked the Pharisees, "You leave the commandment of God, and hold fast human traditions" (Mark 7:8, adapted). Those traditions were once expressions of keeping the commandment of God, but as the original vision dimmed, only the dead letter of the law remained. Tradition can become a seashell, attractive to some but empty of the life that once gave it significance.

The barriers of tradition can be overcome in one of three ways: (1) old traditions can be allowed to die; (2) they can be resurrected and reinterpreted; or (3) new traditions can be created. Most likely all of these approaches will be used depending upon the particular tradition and the life journey of the congregation.

Some traditions will have to die. Their meaning or form is no longer significant to the church in renewal. During the peak period of Dorchester Temple, the deacons wore formal topcoats with tails to serve Communion. As fashions and the general style of the community became more informal, this tradition passed away. When I first came as pastor, we had an annual church fair. As the congregation changed, the priorities for our energies shifted, and the traditional fair died quietly with only a few noticing that we missed it that year. Of course, there are some who feel the loss of familiar traditions. A wise pastor will listen to their sadness, recognize their loss, and shepherd them through the changes. It is also wise to choose carefully which traditions need to die and when. There can be a lot of unnecessary conflict over a pastor trying to kill a tradition that still lives for many older members. The tradition may need to be held onto for a few more years, or it may be a prime candidate for resurrection and renewal.

Many traditions are not understood immediately to a newcomer. Baptism by immersion, for instance, was a ritual evident in its meaning to the first-century Jews. But to a twentieth-century nonbeliever, it is a rather odd practice. With teaching, however, it becomes a powerful drama of one's conversion experience and commitment to Christ. Traditions can be and often need to be reinterpreted for a new generation. They are a part of a rich heritage of faith; they bear our roots and history. Traditions spring out of vision, and if the contemporary visionaries can touch the older vision and find the commonalities, suddenly an old tradition comes alive again. A new setting can also give an old tradition a more varied meaning than it once had. Jesus took the Passover bread and cup and added a new meaning to a millennium-long tradition when he said, "This is my body; this is my blood; do this in remembrance of me."

New traditions can also be created. Traditions are necessary, for they give form, expression, and continuity to the vision. As Dorchester Temple was dealing with integrating black members into what had been a white church, a new tradition was started of singing "Blest Be the Tie That Binds" while holding hands in a big circle after Communion. It affirmed the vision of an inclusive church even when the reality was far from the ideal. As the church has grown, this tradition of almost a decade now has continued to express the members' hope and commitment to one another before God.

Traditions can be barricades along the path of the visionary journey, or they can be stepping-stones. The church in renewal will need to examine each tradition to remove the barricades and rearrange the stepping-stones to help the pilgrim church onward in the most effective way.

Structures

The organizational structures of the church can be either a barrier to renewal or a channel to allow the waters of renewal to flow with creative energy. For many churches in survival mentality, structures are a problem linked strongly to the past, to power cliques, and to traditions. Yet structures are needed to provide form to facilitate decision making and to maintain accountability. How can survivalist churches understand their organizational forms and operations and develop them so that they are assets rather than liabilities to church growth?

All structures are created for a constellation of reasons. Some of the reasons are theological, some traditional, some to meet the practical needs of the local situation, some to respond to the suggestions and requirements of the denominational body. The particular organizational structure is set up to reflect the perceived needs of the congregation and the priorities and values held while trying to meet those needs. Over the years, however, much changes. Theological emphases may shift, and the social makeup of the congregation evolves. The practical needs of the community change. As a result, the structures may no longer be as effective in responding to the church's needs as they once were.

But every structure develops vested interests. People who invest themselves in an organization or identify with a program can have trouble looking critically at the effectiveness and value of their efforts. There is a natural conservative dynamic to preserve the status quo, a dynamic that can often be helpful but which in survivalist churches can also close the door to institutional resurrection. Church structures, like traditions, can become old wineskins that are unable to contain the new wine of the living gospel without breaking. New wineskins are needed, new structures to reflect the current needs, opportunities, and priorities.

No structure is absolutely right or wrong. Structures are

secondary; they are means to the end of serving Christ. A good and useful organizational form in time will become inadequate, so changes need to be made with no feelings of guilt, shame, or failure. Structural change can be as natural a part of growth as a child needing a bigger pair of shoes. Organizations grow and go through phases just as people do, and the structures need to be modified to accommodate the new situation.

A case in point is found in Acts 6. The only organizational structure set up by Jesus was the twelve apostles. As the early church grew, it became more complex, and the structure Jesus left them began to experience the strain of expanded needs. A specific problem developed—inequities in the food distribution for the needy, which highlighted the structural inadequacies. A meeting was held and a new structure was set up. The office of deacon was created to care for the needy among the congregation. The apostolic role was defined more clearly: "prayer . . . and ministry of the word." The church had been slipping into grumbling and dissension due to structural problems, but once they were reorganized, they could get on with pursuing their journeys of worship, nurture, and mission. The story of the overhaul of the organizational form is followed by this progress report: "The word of God increased; and the number of the disciples multiplied greatly in Jerusalem . . ." (Acts 6:7).

Perhaps there could have been a group in the early church who argued against establishing the office of deacon. After all, since Jesus was Lord, didn't he know enough to set things up the way he wanted? If he wanted anybody in the leadership besides apostles, he would have appointed them. No such arguments are recorded in Scripture. Instead, we see a form of Spirit-anointed pragmatism. The problem was addressed directly and creatively, baptized in prayer, and the new structure was filled with people known for being "of good repute, full of the Spirit and of wisdom" (Acts 6:3). Rather than making any particular organizational model sacrosanct, a future-oriented church would benefit from adopting the Spirit-anointed pragmatism demonstrated in this early church crisis.

Dorchester Temple had a structure in 1978 that served well for a church with a stable established membership. It had two major boards (an executive board and diaconate), with all the committees being subcommittees of the executive board. That meant organizationally that to serve on any decision-making body, a person had to be elected to one of the top positions in the congregation. That was no problem when everyone had known everyone else for years. The problem developed as new people entered the church. They were not given access into the flow of decision making until they had earned enough trust to go the top, which can be quite a wait. Furthermore, the small circle of people who served on the boards had so much seniority in the church that nobody was about to ask them to step down to make room for newcomers. The result was that the structure blocked the development of renewal by not allowing newcomers to exercise gifts of leadership and take responsibility for their new church home. People could be attracted to the worship services, but their path into the planning and processes of the church was barred. No malice was intended; it was a structural problem that set up dynamics working against renewal.

The problem was resolved in two stages. The first stage was a minor tinkering with the structure, which had major implications. In changing the bylaws I had only one goal: to bring newcomers into the process. The change was made to open up the committees to the membership at large. Only the chair of each committee would serve on the executive board, along with the church officers and a few at-large members. The impact was immediate and significant. The number of people involved in the decision making doubled, including many folks who have never been involved before. The committees had been mere paper entities because the small circle of people who did everything just didn't have time to make them work. After the bylaws were changed, the committees began to fire up and expand the fellowship experiences and ministry of the church, for the people who served on them had the committees' tasks as their primary concern within the church.

Trying to change the bylaws, even in a minor way, is viewed in some survivalist churches as a threat to the little that remains. Structural change that is done confrontationally is bound to create resistance, for it conveys a spirit of accusation rather than a perspective of normal growth and problem solving. Though I had one goal clearly set in my mind, I listened to the felt needs of the people on the board. They felt overworked; they felt they had too many meetings; they felt others weren't carrying their fair share of the load. After listening to the feelings of frustration, we began to explore various ways that those issues could be addressed, looking for simple solutions, small steps that didn't throw out everything familiar. This positive approach led to the change in bylaws in the first year of my pastorate and opened the door for renewal in the organizational structure.

Bylaw changes can be booby traps that blow up in the face of the visionary pastor. Another church I know tried to make a change to allow new members quicker access to the church boards. The bylaws change was turned into a power struggle, some older members perceiving it as an effort to muscle them out. They called members who were still on the rolls but had moved away, and when the church meeting was held, all these inactive friends of the opponents of the change cast their votes for the status quo. The pastor left shortly after along with many new families who were put off by such a flagrant power play to lock them out of the church of which they longed to be a part. There is probably much to this story that an outsider would never know, but in the end the process of renewal was set back at least five years if not far more.

The second stage of our organizational renewal took place after the vision had taken hold in the congregation and the participation of decision making had broadened to include people from every segment of the congregation. We made a dramatic total overhaul of our church structure, moving away from two boards to a one-board system, changing the relationships and descriptions of the committees, and setting a completely different course for the organizational process. This second-phase change grew out of the renewed vision of the church and the expression of that vision in the new covenant. We tried to create a structure that would concretely express and advance the vision. Each structural component was related to the covenant by name or description. There was broad participation in the process of developing the new bylaws, much discussion, analysis, reworking, discarding, and finally approving. When it was done, we had a structure that had significance to us and that would open up possibilities for growth in the future.

What we conceived on paper was far more elegant than what really happened in our congregation. Some committees were strong and fleshed out their components of the covenantal vision in creative ways. Other committees fell stillborn from the nominating committee report. Churches breaking out of survival mentality don't move forward in formation like a well-rehearsed military unit. So much has decayed that it is more like the process of rebuilding a cellar-dwelling sports team. Each year some wise draft picks and trades add a little more strength until finally enough quality players are in place to make a contender. But even then there are usually some weaknesses that occasionally bring trouble. The church leaders need to work at rebuilding with a long-range view. Some committees may just have to lie dormant to pour the limited energies into developing a quality effort in another area. The old structures were often formed for larger congregations with many more active members than there are presently. If a church tries to revive its Sunday school, get small groups going for adults, establish a vital youth group, rehab the building, develop the finances, increase visitation, expand mission involvement, add programs for the social needs in the community, and revive the worship services all at once, it is sure to end up burning out the pastor and anyone else who tries to take on so many challenges. Triage decisions need to be made prayerfully and openly. Some committees will have to die; our flower committee wilted! Other committees will have to stagger on thanks to one or two competent leaders who will hold the work together on their own. Still others may be ripe for extra pastoral intervention and the investment of new leaders developed in the congregation. A bright spot can develop; then as leaders are strengthened and supported by a growing circle of other participants, the focus can be shifted to another area. I worked intensively for a couple of years with our finance committee. When new leadership was developed, I backed off and put more energies into the Christian education and missions committee which had been struggling. It can seem like one is juggling balls, trying to keep committees or programs from crashing to the ground; but as the vision spreads in the congregation, the renewal will spread organizationally if the channel is prepared for it.

Buildings

Church buildings can be a bane or a blessing. For most survivalist churches, they are a millstone around their necks even though the buildings are cherished places full of hallowed memories. The problem is that years of decline are reflected in the buildings as well as in the people. As the financial base shrinks, the costs of upkeep grow proportionately greater. These costs accelerate if the building is an older structure where major systems can be expected to need repair or renovation. Programs also decline, so the various rooms in the church are not used as frequently or perhaps not at all. When a congregation of under one hundred members is left with a building built for five hundred or one thousand, the result is a crushing financial and maintenance burden. For renewal to take place, the building issues will have to be dealt with creatively.

One critical choke point for buildings is energy use, especially in the northern states with high winter heating bills. Heating massive sanctuaries for a handful of worshipers is poor stewardship and courts financial disaster. Many old buildings have large windows, no weather stripping, no insulation, high ceilings, and old, inefficient furnaces. A church looking at renewal would do well to start with energy issues because there is quick financial payback. Money invested in conservation leads directly to savings on fuel bills. At Dorchester Temple we consumed over 7,200 gallons of fuel oil in the winter of 1978–79. The following year we began to take steps toward conservation and greater heating efficiency. Volunteers began to install weather stripping around the large windows. Storm windows were installed. Our 55- to 85-degree thermostats were replaced with 45- to 75-degree thermostats, allowing us to keep most of the building just warm enough to keep the pipes from freezing. Then four men in the church learned how to blow insulation into the roof and filled our rafters with a twelve-inch blanket of fire-retardent paper wool. Some of these measures cost quite a bit of money, but we took out loans to cover the cost. Loans for weatherization could actually be viewed as investments, which requires some long-range vision, but the pay-back periods can be calculated with some precision so that even timorous trustees can see the wisdom of such efforts. In less than two winters we had recouped all the expenses with savings on our fuel bills. Our oil consumption was down to under 3,200 gallons, a 56 percent reduction! Now every winter the money that once went up the chimney and through the windows can go toward ministry.

One energy-related change was our use of space. We moved our worship services out of the main sanctuary to a side room from the Sunday after Christmas to Palm Sunday. There were benefits to compensate for the loss of the more beautiful, spacious setting for worship. The move created more intimacy by bringing us closer together. Instead of ninety people scattered among pews intended for four hundred, we had ninety people trying to find seats among the one hundred and twenty chairs set up. Though some members did not like the move, others enjoyed the side room better than the sanctuary. The savings were a big boost until the winter came that our growing congregation could no longer fit in the side room. Our return to the sanctuary throughout the winter was a joyful sign of growth.

Space in churches with declining congregations is seldom used except on Sunday. Rentals can be one way to expand the people and financial base supporting the building. Space can be rented to another congregation, perhaps a new ethnic church that doesn't have enough resources for its own building. Rooms can be rented for organizations that need offices or meeting places during the week.

The difficulty in renting space is that the church can either grow dependent upon the outside income and no longer face the critical issues that must be dealt with on the road to renewal or the members can feel like strangers in their own place. Larger groups or weekday organizations can "take over," and resentment can set in among the church members. These problems can be eased if the church takes a long-range approach. No commitment should be made that will preclude future growth and program expansion for the church. Short-term leases leave the future open. The organizations that rent should also have some sort of parallel to the mission of the church. This enables the church to have a sense of identification with their rental groups. Renting space can be a form of ministry, not just a fiscal necessity. The danger is that rentals can become the only form of mission for a church, short-circuiting the renewal of a vision of mission.

Sometimes a building is just so big and expensive for a congregation that it might be advisable to get rid of it. One shrinking Baptist church in Massachusetts was feeling crushed by the weight of their facility, so they traded buildings with a growing Assembly of God church that was bursting the seams of its smaller sanctuary. Both churches benefited. The Assembly of God church continued to grow now that it had room for its expansion. The Baptist church got out from under the obligation to deal with its mammoth structure and could focus on spiritual concerns and church growth. A new sense of vision developed and renewal sprang up. Instead of withering away, that congregation once again is vitally serving the Lord.

Survival mentality looks at building issues with a crisis attitude, staggering on from one set of bills to the next, from one patch-up job to the next. For renewal to break loose, the people responsible for the building need to develop a long-range perspective, seeing all that needs to be done and prioritizing so that renovation can proceed in a coherent fashion. As the renewal takes hold, the congregation will be better able to afford the necessary work on the building. What used to be a millstone gradually returns to being a resource for ministry. Instead of prompting feelings of despair, the sight of the grand old church once again brings joy to the heart.

9

Barriers to Renewal: Old Attitudes

The barriers to renewal covered in this chapter are not problems requiring a technical fix or structural tinkering. These barriers are within peoples' hearts and wedged into their relationships with one another. They are sinful attitudes that need confession, repentance, forgiveness, and healing. Issues surrounding church buildings, organizational structures, and traditions can often trigger the expressions of these attitudinal problems. Discussions of music can be the tripwire for racism to explode in the congregation. A proposed change in the bylaws can inspire the power cliques to rise (or sink) to their pride-filled worst. A decision about spending money to paint the fading fellowship hall can set off the divisiveness between "the mission party" and "the building party." If renewal is to break forth then, not only will the issues of wineskins need to be addressed but also the issue of human hearts. Sinful attitudes will need to be purged. The word of the Lord given to Solomon applies to churches today: "If my people who are called by my name humble themselves, and pray and seek my face, and turn from their wicked ways, then I will hear from heaven, and will forgive their sin and heal their land" (2 Chronicles 7:14). Healing is conditional upon turning from our wicked ways. Three particular wicked ways that need our repentance are pride of power, divisiveness, and racism.

Pride of Power

Pride of power is a sinful attitude that can creep into some of the most loving and dedicated of God's people. Most people get into positions of power in the church not by vicious ladder climbing but by being servants, working steadfastly in the church over the years. They earn peoples' trust and are willing to shoulder responsibility. However, the famous dictum "Power corrupts, and absolute power corrupts absolutely" is valid in the church as well as in politics. Without careful and constant vigilance, holding a position of authority in the church can lead to a spirit of pride that dominates and "lords it over" others. The pride of power can be masked by heavy layers of spirituality, by expressions of love for the Lord and love for the church. But telltale signs can be picked up by the discerning eye and ear. People falling into this attitude consider their dedication to the church as at a higher level than that of the other members. Nobody gives more than they do. Their giving to the church, however, has strings attached, a subtly communicated condition: just so long as things are done my way. Pride can also use the threat of withdrawal, which to a survivalist church is threatening to hammer the final nail into the coffin.

When a key individual or family or small circles of friends control the power in the church and strive to dominate, then the church is in serious trouble. The winds of renewal may blow, but unless their pride of power is removed, the renewal will die. All the efforts of a pastor or a visionary lay person are stifled because he or she presents a center of vitality that is not under the control of the power clique. The clique members block the moving of the Spirit unless they can control it in some fashion. As a result, the people who are most influential in the church become the greatest problem. The church declines around them and can't turn around because of their iron grip on the decision-making process.

These leaders gone sour are like dictators who will let their country disintegrate into chaos rather than step aside from their position of power. The church will close before people with this sin allow another person or group to set the course.

However, there is an alternative, for Christ, the true Lord of the church, can change human hearts. Survivalist churches on the road to renewal can see pride of power defeated, either by conversion or confrontation. Conversion is the way of greatest joy, healing, and power, but if people in control won't humble themselves, a purifying confrontation must take place at some point.

Since pride of power is a condition of the human heart, a change of heart is needed. Though a leader may have accepted Christ as Savior and Lord, there is a further need of repentance and conversion. Pride of power must be removed and servanthood embraced. Exclusive claims must be set aside and a spirit of inclusiveness adopted. Rather than seeking their own way, the leaders must humble themselves to seek Christ's way. Even Jesus our Lord prayed "not my will, but thine, be done" (Luke 22:42). This attitude needs to grow in the hearts of the leaders for renewal to burst forward.

How do hearts change, though, especially for people who have been entrenched in power for years or even decades? Obviously this is the work of the Spirit, for nobody can change another person. We can aid the Spirit's work by careful and consistent teaching on themes of servanthood and the lordship of Christ. In one-on-one conversations, teaching can be specifically applied and modeled. A pastor could help redefine the goals of successful leadership. Rather than holding power, successful leadership develops others to take over the work. For example, Saul was threatened by God's anointed successor, David, much to everyone's sorrow. Saul's leadership could be contrasted to the leadership of Elijah, who heeded God's call to develop Elisha as his successor in the prophetic ministry. The example of Barnabas giving Paul a chance and John Mark a second chance is another positive image of servanthood leadership. Leaders who are genuinely children of God will respond to the loving correction of the Spirit even if they have fallen prey to the pride of power. Most church leaders do have hearts for Christ, but survival mentality has taken its toll in reducing their trust in God and in God's moving through people. As these leaders grow into servanthood, their gifts and knowledge can be used with even greater effectiveness and power. Their pride of power is crucified with Christ to be raised up as humble power centered in the Spirit.

There may be leaders, however, whose hearts are so hardened that they will not budge. They have inflated egos that are fed by their dominance of others, and they are unwilling to sacrifice that dominance for Christ, for the growth of the church, or for their own spiritual well-being. So at some point confrontation becomes necessary.

Acts 8:4-24 tells the story of Simon Magus. When he saw the power of Philip, Peter, and John to heal the sick, drive out demons, and bestow the Holy Spirit, he asked to buy into their access to power. He had known the power of the magician, a manipulator of perceptions to impress others, and he sought the power of God to expand his own egotistical enterprise. But God's power was a gift to be used for the healing and salvation of people, not for personal aggrandizement. Peter's words were harsh but utterly necessary. "Your silver perish with you because you thought you could obtain the gift of God with money! You have neither part nor lot in this matter, for your heart is not right before God" (Acts 8:20-21).

A blunt confrontation like Peter had with Simon might be necessary to overcome those with the pride of power who block the renewal of the church. The confrontation requires perceptive timing, for ugly as it is, there is a power showdown involved. A pastor who confronts too soon will shortly be looking for another church. But if the foundation is laid by working with people who are responsive to the Lord's vision, a base is built in the congregation of people excited about pressing on to the future; then a confrontation can be fruitful. The person in power is like an old politician whose machine is no longer in touch with the new political realities and who is upset in the primaries because the base is no longer there. Renewal will pass by the old guard which clings to power without using it for the service of Christ.

Is such a view cruel or unloving? If those seeking renewal succumb to the definitions that apply to the prideful leadership and their perceptions, then their own spirits will be corrupted. They will be seeking the power itself and not the Lord. They will end up merely replacing one regime with another of the same spirit. But if with humility, compassion, and steadfastness in seeking Christ they press on, a confrontation can be viewed as a way to life for someone in spiritual danger. The person with pride of power is in grave danger. Confrontation may be the stern moment needed to pierce the hardness of heart with the gospel. Peter told Simon, "Repent therefore of this wickedness of yours, and pray to the Lord that, if possible, the intent of your heart may be forgiven you. For I see that you are in the gall of bitterness and in the bond of iniquity" (Acts 8:22-23). Simon's response was one that gave him a new beginning, "Pray for me to the Lord, that nothing of what you have said may come upon me" (Acts 8:24). Those leaders in our churches with pride of power may need a confrontation for the well-being of their own souls, so with love and compassion the hard word must be said.

But what if they will not repent? We need to be willing to let people go. Like defeated politicians, they may drift away, slip off to other churches. They may storm off in ugly scenes of bitterness and accusations. But the primary value is the renewal of the church, the growth of the kingdom of God, not the pampering of bruised egos. If people threaten to withdraw themselves or their financial support, their bluff should be called, for their spirit is a barrier to renewal. Their money isn't worth the price of their loyalty. If they are not open to God's conviction, then their loss, even though it may be traumatic in the short run, in the long run will prove to be a blessing. Renewal and pride of power cannot go together, so ultimately a church must choose which will hold sway.

Racism

Many churches in survival mentality are in places of ethnic transition. White urban neighborhoods have experienced the influx of black, Hispanic, or Asian people. The "white flight" of the fifties and sixties spurred the decline of many urban churches who did not encourage or welcome the newcomers to their neighborhoods. Now, these same dynamics of population shifts and prejudice are being experienced in churches besides the old, white, urban congregations. White suburban churches are facing rising numbers of minorities as affordable housing in cities disappears. The urban issues are now suburban issues. Black congregations are having to deal with growing Hispanic and Asian populations in what were once all-black communities. The prejudice they have experienced themselves is sometimes reflected onto the new minorities in their neighborhoods. For traditional black churches who have gained so much cultural support and identity through their homogeneity, the challenge of becoming multicultural is very threatening. For all the progress made since the days of the civil rights movement, racism and prejudice are still alive and tenaciously rooted in American churches, especially the white churches. They put a tremendous roadblock in the way of renewal. Churches sinking into survival mentality will have little hope of breaking out unless they deal creatively with their prejudice.

In the early church prejudice was a major issue. The division of Jews and Gentiles was ethnically, culturally, and religiously profound. In Galatians 2, Paul recounts how Peter and Barnabas broke off eating with Gentile Christians because of pressure from their Jewish brothers. Prejudice split the fellowship of the church, and Paul's rebuke took the issue to the core of the gospel. In Ephesians 2, Paul speaks of the essential oneness between all Christians through the cross of Christ:

> For he is our peace, who has made us both one, and has broken down the dividing wall of hostility, by abolishing in his flesh the law of commandments and ordinances, that he might create in himself one new humanity in place of the two, so making peace, and might reconcile us both to God in one body through the cross, thereby bringing the hostility to an end. And he came and preached peace to you who are far off and peace to those who were near (Ephesians 2:14-17, adapted).

To refuse to worship alongside brothers and sisters from different cultures and races, extending no mutual respect to one another and not allowing for their unique contribution and styles to be expressed, is to tear Jesus apart. It is an affront to the cross of Christ.

Much is made in the church growth movement of the "homogeneous unit." There is a strong measure of utilitarian truth to the principle of maintaining homogeneous units for the sake of growth. But there is also a price to be paid. In settings of population shifts, homogeneity lets prejudice reign. It lets churches die, and it gives no witness to the community about a Christ who transcends culture. People are not reconciled by the gospel, but rather by common neighborhood issues such as a proposed highway that threatens black and white alike or crime that victimizes everyone. Ethnocentric versions of Christianity develop, and they may grow quickly, but such churches are doomed to disaster when population shifts occur. They will have a heyday in times of stability but will face deep struggles when blacks, Hispanics, Haitians, Italians, Indo-Chinese,

Chinese, Koreans, or any of the ethnic groups that make up our country move in next door. They are congregations of shallow soil, where the seed springs quickly up but then withers in the hot sun of social change (Mark 4:5-6).

Prosperous congregations in homogeneous suburbs (racially or economically) can avoid these issues by virtue of their isolation, but survivalist churches in transitional neighborhoods must face up to the sins of racism and the call of the gospel for reconciliation. Then the biblical vision of the body of Christ spells hope. Antioch was the urban center where the church became cosmopolitan. It had Jews, Greeks, blacks, and probably a few other ethnic groups. Together they had such a vital fellowship that they developed an identity among the nonbelievers that showed where their identity truly lay; in Antioch they were first called "Christians" (Acts 11:26). The Antioch church was as heterogeneous as they come, and they were a large congregation with Holy Spirit-led vision. God chose them to be the first sending church of a genuine missionary effort. Survivalist churches in transitional neighborhoods need not despair, but can rejoice, for they are located in prime territory to lift up the name and gospel of Jesus Christ, if only they can turn aside from their sins of racism.

Developing ethnocentric Christianity may be good for increasing numbers in a church, but it is not good discipleship. Jesus, in his Great Commission, instructed his followers to make disciples of all nations, "teaching them to observe all that I have commanded you . . ." (Matthew 28:20). He let people such as the rich young ruler choose to walk away when they were not willing to sacrifice their sin for the sake of the kingdom. Racism and obedience to Christ are mutually exclusive. The Lord who lifted up the despised Samaritan as the example for love of neighbor will not tolerate a church that wishes to ignore or retain its bigotry.

How then is the church to overcome racism? In one sense we probably never will. Racism is not a condition like smoking where you either do or you don't. When smokers quit, they don't smoke, simple as that, though there may be a lot of personal struggle involved. Racism is more subtly entwined in our hearts, minds, and institutions. A converted wife beater may restrain the explosions of violence in his life, but the pain, the rage, the will to dominate may be more difficult to get at. It may be easy to stop the externals of overt racism—racial slurs and jokes, unequal representation at leadership levels, equal recognition. The covert manifestations of racism are much more difficult to recognize let alone repent of. Cultural stereotypes, unawareness of the different world views and value systems of others, feelings of superiority of one's own culture and the ways these perspectives are expressed in our institutional lives, how we do business, how we conduct worship, how we make decisions—all these subtle forms of racism lurk in the most caring white people and churches. To remove racism is not a one-time massive effort, but a lifelong journey needing humility and grace. A renewed church in a multicultural setting must undertake this journey, and their conscious, deliberate undertaking is a sign of hope.

Racism has to be called the sin that it is, openly, explicitly, and from the pulpit. When Jesus demanded the name of the demons tormenting the Gadarene demoniac, he took power over them. Exposing racism releases some of its power, at the very least in not letting it operate in the hiddenness of our subconsciousness and cultural ignorance or collective conspiracy of silence. Racism should be dealt with in sermons and in Bible studies with more than a superficial treatment. Paul's words about the reconciling power of the cross in Ephesians 2:11-22 provide a deeply theological basis for overcoming racism. Acts 10 tells the more personalized story of God confronting Peter with his own prejudice, then sending him to bring the gospel to Cornelius, the first Gentile whom the church had to embrace as one of the family. The struggle of Peter and the church in Jerusalem reflects many of the same struggles that people experience today in facing their own prejudice. Galatians 2 and Acts 6 present the church wrestling with the practical issues of prejudice— eating together and just distribution of resources. The Bible speaks to the multiple levels of our lives where racism has entwined itself. The vision of the reconciling power of the cross can always be held up to provide the challenge and the grace to press on in the painful journey of confronting this sin.

Perhaps the most effective way to counter racism initially is to develop face-to-face encounters, getting people to work, study, and pray together. Small groups centered around Bible study or a shared mission can help people break down some of their stereotypes and get to know others as Bill or Peter or Ruby or Kathy, not as "a white" or "a black." In one mixed Bible study group, a white woman commented about the black women in the group, "I didn't know they were so spiritual! They put me to shame." Obviously, she still had a long way to go, but through the face-to-face encounter of the small group she was having her stereotype shaken and was beginning to recognize God's presence in people different from herself. Such individual relationships that develop into friendships and bonds of trust don't solve the problems, but they do move those in the relationship beyond the limits of their racist roots.

If the church has more than one culture present, the cultural diversity can be celebrated as part of the church's life of fellowship and worship. This both honors and teaches respect for the various expressions of God's image through our different cultural prisms. Our church delighted in an annual international harvest dinner at Thanksgiving where we made dishes that highlighted our various ethnic heritages. We also laughed over our clapping to music in worship. Blacks clapped off the beat; whites on the beat. When the result was chaos, we would acknowledge the humorousness of our diversity and then choose a rhythm most appropriate to the style of music we were singing. By doing this we recognized and respected our differences yet found unity in worship.

However, much of racism cannot be handled by ethnic potlucks, clapping off the beat, or having blacks and whites together in a Bible study. A church serious about dealing with its racism in the context of building the reconciled body of Christ will be willing to do the more painful and threatening work of intentionally digging deep and exploring institutionalized forms of racism.

Some issues cannot be easily analyzed but must be tackled in good faith. Our Sunday school was made up of almost all black students taught by black teachers. In such a mixed church an all-black Sunday school raised a lot of legitimate questions regarding racism. Were the black children being disowned by the whole church and left only for the blacks to nurture in their spiritual development? Part of the issue was demographics; the older white families had seen their children grow up and move away. Most of the younger white families had children too young for Sunday school. Only three white families had kids of Sunday school age, so obviously the Sunday school students would be mainly black children. White families who didn't send their children raised issues about their children not enjoying Sunday school and not wanting to make their attendance compulsory. Some black leaders, however, felt that racism was at the root, especially since only one or two whites were teaching. Here is where communication, mutual understanding, and risk taking are vital to keep a church growing together rather than splintering into recrimination and bitterness. Everyone involved had legitimate issues and concerns, and the overall situation certainly did not reflect genuine oneness. Through a lot of talking together at leadership levels, through occasional sermon illustrations and once even a direct statement about the lack of white participation in our Sunday school, and through people taking risks of reaching out to other members of the congregation, some progress was made. A few more whites began to teach or provide some support services, but the struggle still goes on. Racism often presents itself not openly but mixed up with a host of other issues and problems that make resolution more complex and difficult.

Complexity and difficulty are no excuses for not working at removing racism and its effects in the church. To grapple with the more tangled issues, the church may want to turn to outside help, to consultants skilled in training on racism or multicultural relationships. Seminars, workshops, or retreats for people in leadership may give the members new understanding of the issues so that they can negotiate more just and equitable structures and processes in the church. This stage of the journey requires enough trust and common commitment to the vision of the church that the risks can be taken. As the renewal picks up steam, the church should begin planning and setting goals for taking on the thornier issues that will restrict their further growth.

Racism blocks the work of renewal, but confronting this sin in its individual and corporate expressions provides an opportunity for the people in the church to experience the grace of God together. To confess, know pain, receive forgiveness, come to new understandings, cry, and laugh forges deep bonds. Dealing with our racism individually or corporately is a lifelong struggle, but as the vision of the reconciled body of Christ is held up, the people move a bit closer to living in its reality.

Divisiveness

Divisiveness is an attitude of the "flesh" that can be a result of pride of power, racism, or a host of other pernicious causes. Frequently in small churches divisiveness can be seen in a lingering feud between individuals or families that began with some long-ago slight that has never been forgiven. Issues may be debated, doctrinal stands made, matters of principle proclaimed, but at the heart of the conflict is a shattered relationship. If the parties involved are in the mainstream of church life, their conflict spills over and pollutes the entire congregation.

The apostle Paul was familiar with divisiveness. In Galatians 5:19-21 (NIV), he warns us,

> The acts of the sinful nature are obvious: sexual immorality, impurity and debauchery; idolatry and witchcraft; hatred, discord, jealousy, fits of rage, selfish ambition, dissensions, factions, and envy; drunkenness, orgies, and the like. I warn you, as I did before, that those who live like this will not inherit the kingdom of God.

Surrounded by all the sins repugnant to most church folks is the longer list of sins evidenced in churches torn by dissension. And just as individuals who stubbornly cling to these aspects of the sinful nature cannot inherit the kingdom of God, churches that allow divisiveness to go unchecked will not break out of survival mentality. They will only sink deeper into the mire of bitterness, resentment, and recrimination.

A prime example was the church in Corinth. Paul wrote, "For it has been reported to me by Chloe's people that there is quarreling among you, my brothers and sisters. What I mean is that each one of you says, 'I belong to Paul,' or 'I belong to Apollos,' or 'I belong to Cephas,' or 'I belong to Christ' " (1 Corinthians 1:11-12, adapted). All through the letter we see the specific issues that marked their falling out from one another: lawsuits, greed during church suppers, speaking in tongues, sexual ethics, food offered to idols. They seem a church looking for a reason to fight. But at the beginning of his letter, Paul confronts their basic spiritual immaturity:

> But I, brothers and sisters, could not address you as spiritual people, but as people of the flesh, as babes in Christ. I fed you with milk, not solid food; for you were not ready for it; and even yet you are not ready, for you're still of the

flesh. For while there is jealousy and strife among you, are you not of the flesh, and behaving like ordinary people? For when one says, "I belong to Paul," and another, "I belong to Apollos," are you not merely people? (1 Corinthians 3:1-4, adapted).

Who is right on a particular issue doesn't matter. Nobody is right, everybody is wrong, for they are all behaving in a way that doesn't reflect the mind of Christ or the way of the Spirit. They are operating out of their sinful nature.

In a divisive church a pastor is forced to walk amid an emotional minefield; one false step can lead to an explosion and possibly another pastoral casualty. It is very easy to get sucked into taking sides in a conflict. Paul had a group that claimed his inspiration, "I belong to Paul" (1 Corinthians 1:12). But he refused to be drawn even into their party in the dispute: "Was Paul crucified for you? Or were your baptized in the name of Paul?" (1 Corinthians 1:13). Instead of joining any side, even the side one agrees with, church leaders must press on to the deeper issue, the spirit of divisiveness. Unless this is overcome at its root, no resolution of the more immediate issues can be satisfactory. One side or the other would "win," but the body of Christ as a whole would lose.

Overcoming divisiveness takes a lot of prayer, love, forgiveness, and patience. A leader must take care to communicate both love and respect for individuals as well as consistent refusal to join in accusations and undercutting of others. Feelings can be acknowledged without being accepted as the whole truth.

One way the church can organizationally deal with divisiveness is in boards and committees and other meetings for church business. The form used for planning can become a tool for building unity and shared responsibility. In many churches democratic processes are followed, leading to a vote where the majority position becomes the governing one. Divisiveness will only gain more fuel for its fires through democratic process. A planning process that is inclusive in participation and strives for consensus will break down the divisions and give a common goal or program.

Inclusiveness in planning can be achieved by asking the people in the group to envision the future; how would they like the church to be in one year or five years? Divisiveness tends to be rooted in the past, so a new environment is created by getting people to look toward a future in which they will all have a stake. Through brainstorming, encouraging everyone to add a part to the vision, a more comprehensive goal develops rather than the one "yes or no" issue fought over by the factions. People can begin to see their common desires and concerns, and by sharing the process of shaping the plan, they share the ownership. Training on inclusive planning processes would be a wise investment for a pastor and other key church leaders, not just for their increased technical skill, but for the cause of building unity as they pursue God's vision for the future.[1]

For some divisive churches a project can be unifying if it can be left unlinked to this faction or that party. A church cleanup day, a new mission project, or a social event can become an opportunity to bring people together to build common ties that eventually become deeper than the differences. I observed one fragmented church whose pastor used a comprehensive building remodeling program to pull together a congregation that had been torn by bickering for years. A key ingredient to the success of such ventures is that they are not identified with any single element of the church but transcend the pet projects and favored axes to grind. Furthermore, the most effective projects call the church toward a new future so that the eyes of the people are lifted beyond the narrow confines of their conflict.

---

[1]A generic planning process has been developed by the Center for Constructive Change. "Plannaging: Planning and Managing for Change" is a conceptual model that can be applied to many areas of individual and corporate life, including churches. The Center is available for consultation and training. Contact them at The Center for Constructive Change, 16 Strafford Avenue, Durham, NH 03824.

The sinful nature is overcome by the work of the Holy Spirit in human hearts, so healing divisiveness is a work of God. Projects to unify, developing inclusive processes and consensus decision making, by themselves, will be technical fixes and prove inadequate. Human efforts need to be preceded, accompanied, and followed by prayer. The vision of God reminds us of God's presence in the church to bring people together for God's purpose, so in prayer the divisive spirit can be lifted up. It is a concern taken up by Jesus in his prayer before going to the cross:

> "I do not pray for these only, but also for those who believe in me through their word, that they may all be one; even as thou, Father, art in me, and I in thee, that they also may be in us, so that the world may believe that thou hast sent me. The glory which thou hast given me I have given to them, that they may be one even as we are one, I in them and thou in me, that they may become perfectly one, so that the world may know that thou hast sent me and hast loved them even as thou hast loved me" (John 17:20-23).

We believe that the Holy Spirit will be actively engaged in this work so pressing in God's own heart.

Prayer can also be a means to build a sense of identification with people outside one's own circle. Dorchester Temple had a problem with being fragmented; there were so many projects going on, so many small groups, that we often struggled to maintain a sense of togetherness. Though divisiveness itself was not the issue, one of the ways we prayed could be helpful in a factionalized church. When we prayed, we sometimes required that people not pray out loud for any group they were directly involved in, but only for those in which they did not participate. It was very moving to hear and be supported by the prayers of those outside one's particular group or ministry. Praying for one another builds unity, for we cannot bring our divisiveness before God and expect to hold onto it. Through our praying Jesus' own prayer moves closer to fulfillment.

Powers, Perseverance, and Promise

*T*he journey out of survival mentality is fraught with trials and difficulties. The way is never neat; rather it is littered with false starts, failed programs, and frustrated dreams. The struggle is intense, and often the vision bearer and other people of good faith are casualties. This chapter will address some of the issues that arise in the experience of struggle involved in breaking out of survivalism, leading finally to the promise of the Lord Jesus Christ, which is our guiding beam of light through the fog of despair and defeatism.

The Powers

We can examine churches in survival mentality through sociological or psychological frameworks, through the perspective of group process and organizational planning, or from a theology of the church. However, there is another dimension to the situation of survivalist churches that must be recognized and confronted. In Ephesians 6:12 Paul writes, "For we are not contending against flesh and blood, but against the principalities, against the powers, against the world rulers of this present darkness, against the spiritual hosts of wickedness in the heavenly places." There are powers at work not only in the world but in the church, powers that cannot be totally accounted for by group psychology or strange combinations of chance. The Bible speaks of spiritual beings and forces that are not altogether clear in nature but that are encountered in the struggle to do God's will in the world. The "powers and principalities" have vested interests in the status quo and are resistant to the creative work of the Holy Spirit and the people of God for renewal.

These spiritual vested interests can manifest themselves in the group psyche through the despair and unbelief that can be ingrained in a group of people who individually may be full of faith. Just as the breaking out of this mind-set is more than mere positive thinking but is the work of the Holy Spirit, the iron grip of survival mentality is reinforced by the powers and principalities. The group mind-set has a life of its own, and there is tremendous pressure to conform to the subtle and persistent dominant perspective.

Such a manifestation of the powers can easily be viewed as no more than group psychology, but there are other manifestations of the powers at work. At Dorchester Temple we were struck with the high incidence of traumatic events surrounding key moments in the renewal process. People were mugged, laid off their jobs, or became ill in bunches. Just when the movement toward new life in the church was demanding the most challenging steps of faith and hope, key members were faced with the additional stresses of fear and anxiety for their own physical safety and well-being. I don't claim to have a clear understanding of demonology, but we are convinced that perverse powers were at work beyond our human sensibilities, a conclusion the apostle Paul would certainly have understood and affirmed.

In the face of these powers the call is to wage spiritual warfare. "Finally, be strong in the Lord and in the strength of his might. Put on the whole armor of God, that you may be able to stand against the wiles of the devil" (Ephesians 6:10-11). Three of the components of the armor of God are especially suited to the spiritual warfare that occurs in survivalist churches. The shield of faith, "with which you can quench all the flaming darts of the evil one" (Ephesians 6:16), is the lifting up of vision in the face of all the setbacks and stumbles the church experiences. The shield of faith protects with its affirmations of the vision of God, who will lead the church through even its current crisis, no matter what powers are arrayed against it. By faith the church can claim the promise of Christ: "On this rock I will build my church, and the powers of death shall not prevail against it" (Matthew 16:18). The Word of God, which Paul calls the "sword of the Spirit" (Ephesians 6:17), is the offensive weapon. The proclaimed, taught, and applied Word of God is able to drive back the fear and doubt that would drain away the energy of a church being renewed. Paul's final word in spiritual warfare is about prayer: "Pray at all times in the Spirit, with all prayer and supplication. To that end keep alert with all perseverance, making supplication for all the saints" (Ephesians 6:18). When we sensed the growing tide of struggle, within and without, we would gather for special prayer meetings called specifically to engage in spiritual warfare. Our surge of prayer as we entrusted our challenges and crises to God was energized by the Holy Spirit to carry us through those difficult moments. The vision of God, being present and active among us, was both tested and strengthened as we prayerfully passed through the struggles. The powers can be overcome, for as the Scriptures proclaim, "The One who is in you is greater than the one who is in the world" (1 John 4:4, adapted).

Besides the power of God and the power of the spiritual vested interests, there is our own power as human beings to decide whether or not to respond to the call of God. Churches as corporate bodies can make decisions for or against renewal. Evangelists urge their hearers to make decisions for Christ, and vision bearers are calling for similar decisions. Instead of a decision regarding one's own personal destiny, the choice impacts the corporate destiny, the future life of the church. As Moses neared death, he presented a choice to the people of Israel:

> "I call heaven and earth to witness against you this day, that I have set before you life and death, blessing and curse; therefore choose life, that you and your descendants may live, loving the LORD your God, obeying his voice, and cleaving to him; for that means life to you and length of days, that you may dwell in the land which the LORD swore to your ancestors, to Abraham, to Isaac, and to Jacob, to give them" (Deuteronomy 30:19-20, adapted).

Churches in survival mentality have a choice to make between life and death. Though they cannot create the new life themselves, they can choose to "cleave to God" and open themselves for the winds of renewal to blow among them. They may choose death instead. The congregation may choose to hold on to the status quo, to live by worn-out traditions, to clutch their fading power, to live in the past. That choice is a decision for death, but God gives them the power to make it. Tragically many churches will choose death. Even as the rich young ruler chose not to surrender his wealth for the call of the gospel and walked sadly away from Jesus (Mark 10:17-22), far too many congregations will turn away from the Lord of the church because they are not willing to give up the old wineskins and old attitudes that hinder renewal. Elijah challenged the people of Israel to make a clear choice: "How long will you go limping with two different opinions? If the LORD is God, follow him; but if Baal, then follow him" (1 Kings 18:21). The limping survivalist churches have the power to decide. To put off the decision is to choose further decline and death, but to commit expectantly their present and future into the hands of God is to enter into the way of new life.

Perseverance

The Bible is full of words such as "perseverance," "long-suffering," "patience," "endurance," "overcoming," and "steadfastness." These are difficult words for us because they assume trouble and struggle, but such is the story of most of our journeys of faith. Breaking out of survival mentality is not an easy process. The church is wandering in a spiritual wasteland, a barren wilderness of hopelessness. The trek to the promised land of renewal stretches one's faith and inner resources to the maximum. To the church of Ephesus, which had drifted away from its first love of Christ and needed to renew its corporate spirit, Jesus promised, "To the one who overcomes I will grant to eat of the tree of life, which is in the paradise of God" (Revelation 2:7, adapted). To the church of Philadelphia, struggling under persecution and poverty, Jesus promised, "The ones who overcome, I will make them pillars in the temple of my God . . ." (Revelation 3:12, adapted). The promise of Christ is extended to the churches caught in survival mentality. If they will overcome their spiritual lethargy and the hardships that intimidate them, Jesus will let them feast upon his new life and make them pillars of his church upon the earth. The key is overcoming, persevering.

To persevere, church leaders, especially vision bearers, need to understand the length of their ministry. Soldiers in Vietnam and World War II had very different tours of duty. In Vietnam soldiers served only for a year, at the end of which they could leave the war and all it entailed to return to noncombat duty. This bred survival mentality among the soldiers. The key was to survive till that final day when they could board the plane and get out of Vietnam. Pastors often adopt this same way of thinking in their small, struggling churches. Their main objective is to somehow muddle through the minimum acceptable amount of time till they get a "good church" or retire. Personal and professional survival become the overriding values, and it is no wonder that their cause is a losing one.

In World War II the soldiers were "in for the duration." They served until victory or defeat came or until they were casualties. The goal was not merely survival but victory; victory was the way to survival. The vision bearer and all who would be a part of the renewal process would do well to think in terms of being "in for the duration." Then perseverance is nurtured because the vision is long-range and comprehensive, not shortsighted and personal.

Even with an attitude of perseverance and a long-term commitment to the church, a pastor can labor for years and see few if any tangible results. Sometimes the church still declines in vitality, attendance, and financial resources. How can a vision bearer endure when nothing positive seems to be happening, when the cry on the lips is "How long, O Lord?"

The pastor can help himself or herself by cultivating a long-term vision, perhaps one that even extends far beyond his or her tenure in that ministry. Since the church is Christ's church, not our own, we all labor for a larger enterprise than any of our own efforts, programs, or influence. If we have a vision that goes beyond the immediate threat to survival, we can labor for goals that may lie beyond our moments on the scene. Paul spoke of sharing in a labor larger than himself. In First Corinthians he writes:

> What then is Apollos? What is Paul? Servants through whom you believed, as the Lord assigned to each. I planted, Apollos watered, but God gave the growth. So neither the one who plants nor the one who waters is anything, but only God who gives the growth. The one who plants and the one who waters are equal, and each shall receive his or her wages according to the labor. For we are God's co-workers; you are God's field, God's building.
>
> According to the grace of God given to me, like a skilled master builder I laid a foundation, and another is building upon it. Let each one take care how he or she builds upon it" (1 Corinthians 3:5-10, adapted).

Churches with survival mentality have the sense of history that illustrates Paul's teaching. Many pastors have served over the years (and their photographs often grace the church like an accusers' gallery in the minds of their struggling successors). Even pastorates of twenty and forty years have faded into the distance. If the church is to persevere and come into a future full of promise, then its leaders need to build with as much awareness of time ahead as of time behind. They are laying new foundations that someone else will build upon. To affirm that fact is a statement of vision.

With a long-range perspective, pastors can set more intermediate goals within a meaningful context. They don't have to "do it all." Their role may not be to preside over the key turning point but to lead the church through a necessary preparatory step. Interim ministers frequently serve in this role, helping the church through one important breakthrough or self-recognition so that the arriving pastor can pick up the journey a little further down the road. The interim pastor immediately preceding me at Dorchester Temple helped the congregation make significant progress integrating black members into the mainstream of church life so that I, as the new pastor, could help the church move from that point forward. He helped reform the youth group and recruited as their leader, a woman who went on to become one of the key leaders in the church. He also instituted the tradition of holding hands in a circle following Communion to sing "Blest Be the Tie That Binds." Many of the people who participated in the earlier stages of the renewal were brought to faith or brought into the church through his ministry. Pastorates or interim pastorates may have as a major objective to "raise one valley" or "lower one mountain" in preparation for the coming day of renewal.

Sometimes pastors may play the frustrating role of Moses leading the people through the wilderness and helping them through their conflicts to develop into a new community. Another may follow who will be the Joshua, the one to lead into the promised land of renewal. Both Moses and Joshua were people of vision, though their places within God's scheme were very different. Having a clear conception of one's role can help a leader persevere through the wilderness years.

As I closed out my pastorate, I met one of the former pastors who had served the church during the turbulent late sixties and early seventies. The nation was being torn apart by war and deceit, parts of Boston burned during riots, and the church continued to be buffeted by white flight and community decline. This pastor had the vision and had ministered faithfully, teaching and modeling reconciliation and outreach during those difficult years. He spoke of a sustaining hope he had that the opportune time would come, and he wanted to hold the church together until then and even prepare it for the renewal ahead. I realized in talking to him that I had been unconsciously standing on his shoulders throughout my ministry. His own vision and labor had made my way a bit easier as he planted seeds that I was later to harvest.

Yet a caution needs to be raised: Don't let your own definition of your role limit what God might do. Don't be too quick to label yourself as a Moses for the wilderness years alone. Be ready for surprise. If we are filled with vision, the renewal may come quicker than even we expect.

While the church is in the wilderness of survival mentality, the vision bearer needs to be nurtured in his or her own spirit. Moses could go on the mountain or into the tabernacle and meet with God directly, but for pastors and other vision bearers, continual spiritual growth and refreshment is not so accessible. Of course, there is the private devotional life, but we have also been made to need corporate worship. "I was glad when they said to me, 'Let us go to the house of the LORD!' " (Psalm 122:1). However, the gladness dissipates when one enters the despair of survivalist churches, which presents a painful dilemma for the pastor and his or her family. How do they keep getting nurtured when their church is dead? From where do they draw living water when their church is in the desert?

Developing a personal support network is crucial. Young pastors would do well to establish a mentoring relationship with an experienced pastor. I often called on a nearby pastor whom I respected for his pastoral work. He became an older brother in ministry to me, providing encouragement, feedback, and guidance. My regional denominational office established a three-year program for new pastors to provide support and continuing education. We met three times a year for day-long retreats. Most of us were in survivalist churches, and by sharing our experiences together, we gained insights to aid our own work and were encouraged to persevere. Just knowing you are not alone is energizing. Clergy associations can meet these needs as well if they are willing to get beyond local competitiveness and business agendas. To face honestly the struggles with survival mentality in the represented churches will require a mutual commitment to honesty and vulnerability. Where pastors have taken the risk, the results are usually satisfying and empowering.

The nurture of one's spirit in worship is often an issue for the pastor and the pastor's family. When the worship life is relatively dead and depressing, some have found it helpful to occasionally attend services at another church to meet their own needs. This can be awkward, but the risks and limitations may be outweighed by the need to be uplifted and spiritually fed. Even visionaries cannot sustain themselves with a famine of worship.

Before the renewal got rolling at Dorchester Temple, my wife and I regularly attended an evening worship service at a church in another denomination. Some people knew we were attending another church; we told them we needed to worship occasionally where I wasn't labeled as the "pastor." Pastors need to be fed, too, and most parishioners could understand that. The situation was artificial, for we could never become a part of the community of the other church. Our community and commitment remained at Dorchester Temple, but if we were to fulfill our task as vision bearers, we had to maintain our own spiritual vitality. Eventually, as the worship life of Dorchester Temple became creative and faith-filled, our need to go elsewhere withered away. Our renewed church was fully our worshiping community.

Different pastors will have varied needs for worship and spiritual nurture. How those needs are best met is a personal matter, but each should feel free and guiltless if he or she chooses to reach out to portions of the body of Christ outside the local congregation. A pastor may face the dangers of being lured away from one's call or succumbing to increased frustration over the home church's shortcomings. However, the fulfillment of the vision bearer's ministry requires spiritual strength and depth that need maintenance and sustenance. Stewardship of who we are is part of our responsibility in the renewal process.

The Promise

The vision God gave Ezekiel of the valley of dry bones was a vision of promise. When God raised up the bones, gave them flesh and breath, and caused them to stand, they had become "a vast army." This was no idle dream, no fainthearted fantasy. God's own integrity was on the line with the promise:

> "You shall know that I am the LORD, when I open your graves, and raise you from your graves, O my people. And I will put my Spirit within you, and you shall live, and I will place you in your own land; then you shall know that I, the LORD, have spoken, and I have done it, says the LORD" (Ezekiel 37:13-14).

God's promise of renewal is a steadying gift to churches in survival mentality. If they allow the vision to be lifted up, if they allow the winds of the Spirit to blow new life into them, if they respond in faith to the call of God, renewal will come. God is looking for those who will bear witness to the divine grace at work in the world, and a renewed church is a testimony that cannot be denied. As God moves, it will be clear that God truly has spoken and has done it.

To the vision bearers who pour out their lives in service of God for renewal, the promise is spelled out in Galatians 6:9, "Let us not grow weary in well-doing, for in due season we shall reap, if we do not lose heart." There will be failures. Programs that were put forth with zeal and high expectations will fizzle. People we hoped would shoulder key responsibilities will move away to more exciting churches. Moments of victory are overshadowed by large unexpected disasters. But if we are sowing to the Spirit, following God's call, and living out the vision of God, church, and mission, the promise of Christ is that we shall reap. A time of harvest will come.

For us to share in that moment, we must not lose our own hope and faith. The promise is that we shall reap "if we do not lose heart." The prophet Habakkuk lived in a time that stretched and tested one's faith. Israel was in survival mentality, feeling like the dry bones in Ezekiel's vision. Habakkuk was given a vision about God's justice but also instructed regarding the time of waiting:

> "Write the vision;
> Make it plain upon tablets,
> so they may run who read it.
> For still the vision awaits its time;
> it hastens to the end—it will not lie.
> If it seems slow, wait for it;
> it will surely come, it will not delay.
> Behold, the ones whose souls are not
> upright in them shall fail,
> but the righteous shall live by their faith"
> —Habakkuk 2:2-4, adapted

The righteous one lives by faith, especially during the in-between time, during the period of waiting and expectancy. As the vision bearers wait for God's renewal to break out in their churches, the challenge is to live by faith. The one who lives by faith in the God of promise will be able to see the vision and run with it, for surely it shall come.

Epilogue: A Celebration

On November 9, 1986, Dorchester Temple Baptist Church celebrated its one hundredth anniversary. While the ninetieth anniversary had been characterized by suppressed question marks and doubts, the centennial was an unabashed and profound celebration. Survival mentality was a part of history. Now the future belonged to the church. New challenges, opportunities, and ministries beckoned.

Former members came to join the present members in a day of worship and celebration. People came from as far as Montana, California, and Florida, as well as the New England states. Five former pastors and Dr. Charles Hendricks, pastor of our mother church, Tremont Temple in downtown Boston, gathered together to lead in worship. One high spot was the Communion service when we spontaneously spoke out the names of those who had died and had shared Communion and ministry with us. As the names were heard one by one, we sensed "the cloud of witnesses" upon whose work we were building.

After the service we had a dinner followed by a program of music and pastoral reflections. Each of the pastors shared memories of his time at the church. We heard a lot of good stories, but even more we were deeply touched by the historical flow of the church's life, the struggles, the breakthroughs. Our musical leaders led in a festival of song, most of it original, which displayed the vitality of our renewed worship and drew us all into the spirit of joyous celebration. As the sun began to set, the program concluded with a slide show. Photographs of people and church events spanning the years were shown as I spoke about the church being the people of God. Our styles and formats may change, people grow and pass on, but the basic ministry of the church endures as Christ moves through God's people. We all left that evening with full hearts and a glow of joy.

That one hundredth anniversary celebration was much more to us than marking a milestone in longevity. It was a time of being made whole, of surprising healing. Former members who had left during days of decline were deeply moved to see the vitality of the renewed church. Their own efforts had not been in vain. The heritage of their life and work at Dorchester Temple was not lost with the closing of another church door but was the living branch from which new life was now growing. New members were moved by a sense of history they had never quite appreciated. They sensed the longer flow of struggle that they had thought new with themselves. The newcomers could share a deeper appreciation of the spiritual heritage of the remnant who had endured through the times of deepest despair and of the former members who had given so much during their own sojourn in the church. Former members, new members, and old members who bridged the chapters of the church's history all experienced a community of faith that brought them great joy. They were even free to weep gently together as they remembered those who had died after giving us all so much love.

The Psalms tell us "weeping may tarry for the night, but joy comes with the morning" (Psalm 30:5). A church with vision believes in God's morning. The day will dawn; joy will spring forth. It was sweet to celebrate together God's gift of a new life.

Appendix: Using This Book for a Group

*T*his appendix is a guide for a group within a church to study, reflect, and pray together about how God is calling them to move into the future. A leadership board (elders, deacons) or a special gathering of leaders across the entire church structure can go through these six sessions to consider seriously their present situation as a church and to open themselves as a community of leaders to God's direction. For churches in survival mentality I would hope such a process would be a significant step in their journey of renewal.

As stated repeatedly in this book, God is the key actor in the drama of renewal. We can only prepare the altar and the sacrifice, but God lights the fire. Therefore, prayer must be a major component of these sessions. Suggestions for prayer are given to help focus the thoughts of the participants and sharpen their sensitivity to God's voice.

Participation by all the members of the group is essential. Community is shaped by each person being willing to take the risk of sharing his or her perspectives, concerns, and hopes. A ground rule must be set to listen respectfully to each person's viewpoint and statement. Whether one agrees or not with what another says is secondary to hearing what is on that person's heart and mind. The facilitator should especially encourage the comments of those who are more reserved and quiet in the group, as their contributions are as vital as anyone else's. Taking risks to be honest and open with one another will lead to greater community among the members, deeper trust, and a more fertile soil for God's harvest to spring forth.

To aid the participatory nature of the group, I would advise that leadership either be rotated or brought in from outside (perhaps a local denominational staff person could help or a renewal consultant be brought in). If the position of group facilitator is rotated each session, then all the members of the group will have more ownership of the process; it won't just be the pastor's project. For renewal to take hold it must be caught by the leaders of the church, so they cannot sit passively through this process and expect it to work. Renewal takes work and commitment by everyone involved.

The six sessions that follow provide suggestions and guidance for the group meetings. However, feel free to follow the leading of the Spirit. Be open to surprises, and don't feel confined by what is written here. Take the time you need to do your work well. May God's blessing and joy be with you in your journey together.

Session 1
Assignment
Read Prologue and Chapter 1 before the session begins.
Group Exercise
Provide everyone with a large piece of paper and crayons or colored markers. Ask people to draw a graph that shows the history of the church, plotting downward and upward periods in the church life. Have them draw pictures to express what was happening in those periods or at turning points in the history. If the group has more than eight people, break up into groups of four or five people each. Ask each individual to tell the others about his or her picture.

Discussion

After all have shown what they drew, gather together and talk about what your church has been through and where it is now in its lifeline. Add input from the Prologue and Chapter 1 to your discussion. Is the church looking forward or backward? What was the high point in the church's history? What changes have been the most threatening? How do you feel about what has been brought out in this session?

Meditation

Have participants close their eyes and use their imagination to see this vision. A person should read Ezekiel 37:1-14 slowly, giving the mind enough time to see and feelings enough time to rise to the surface. After the reading ask people to share what they felt. Where did people identify with the story? What did God's message say to them personally?

Prayer

Encourage many people to pray aloud. Pray specifically about the history of the church that has been discussed today, the feelings that have been voiced, and the concerns people have. Pray for God to move upon the church to raise it up like Israel in Ezekiel's vision. Thank God for the hope of renewal given in the Scriptures. Ask God to energize that hope in your own hearts.

Session 2

Assignment

Read Chapters 2 and 3 before the session begins.

Group Exercise

Pass out paper and pencils to individuals. Ask them to list the three major problems or barriers that they think stand in the way for the church to grow. List them on newsprint or a blackboard, noting the number of people who mention each problem.

Bible Study

Read Numbers 13:25–14:9. What was the full picture the spies saw regarding the Promised Land? Why were the ten so negative? What made Joshua and Caleb different? Did Joshua and Caleb see the same problems as the ten? Why did the problems not deter them from moving ahead?

Discussion

When you look at the issues that face your church, which feeling looms larger: despair, frustration, hope, fear? What makes you feel that way? How does your congregation experience the presence of God together? Is that question hard to answer? Why or why not? What would faith look like if applied to each of the problems you listed? What specific step of faith can you take together?

Prayer

Take time to pray over each issue or problem mentioned. Instead of having one person pray a long prayer about everything on the list, then the next person doing the same thing, have a number of people pray short prayers on the same subject; then change subjects and continue with short topical prayers. After all the concerns and problem areas have been prayed for, have people sit prayerfully with hands on their laps or knees, palms open and up while one person reads Psalm 46. Pray in affirmation and praise that God is with you right now. Close with a commitment to act practically in the faith that God is working in your church.

Session 3

Assignment

Read Chapter 4 before the session begins.

Group Exercise

Work as a group to develop a chart on newsprint or a chalkboard. List each group within the church. Begin with official boards and committees; move on to structured small groups; finish with identifiable clusters of friends. What is the function of each group within the church? What needs do these groups meet for the church and for their members? What is the major issue or concern they bring to the whole church?

Bible Study

Read 1 Corinthians 12:4-7, 12-27. What purposes for the members of the body of Christ are mentioned in this passage (general purposes, not specific tasks)? Give examples of how people or groups can work to fulfill these purposes. How does Paul counter the passivity of many church members? How does Paul counter the attitude that one's own area of church work is most important?

Discussion

Do you feel supported or alone in what you do for the church? What would help you feel more support and affirmation in your task? What are other people saying they need for support? Can you state clearly and fairly the goals and concerns of groups you don't relate to directly? What can be done to meet more adequately the needs and address the concerns stated in this session?

Prayer

Take turns praying for one another and the various groups in the church. Only pray out loud for groups with whom you have no direct participation. Pray for the hopes and needs you have heard expressed. Pray for the growing unity of your church.

Session 4

Assignment

Read Chapter 5 before the session begins.

Group Exercise

Within your local community, what are the needs people have of which you are already aware? Make a list on newsprint or a chalkboard. Do you know of any people in your own church who are affected personally by those issues? Mark which ones. (There may be many folks affected by needs in the community who haven't chosen to let their problems be known to the church folks.) For each need listed, what specific bridge has your church made to reach and welcome that specific group of people? How well is it working?

Bible Study

Read Isaiah 58:1-12. What is the key to renewal in this passage? Why is religious ritual, being active in church, not enough? How can the needy be welcomed into our house, personally or into the church "house?" What kind of actions does God call for as a part of the genuine service of God?

Discussion

Pick one issue on the list drawn up at the beginning of the session. Assign one person to be advocate (not "devil's advocate"!) to feel the needs, concerns, and hopes of a person in that situation. The advocate should respond to suggestions made by the group with as much empathy as possible. What can the church do to reach out to people faced with this issue? What would be most helpful to add in the church's life? What would need to be dropped? What would need to be altered? Where will this person find friends? How will those contacts be made and developed?

Prayer

Pray for the needs of the community that you have discussed. Pray for the Spirit's guidance and direction to open a new door of ministry to the community. In silence let each person covenant with God one step that he or she is willing to take to expand the mission of the church. After a few minutes of silence, ask those who feel led to voice their covenant in prayer. Close, praying for God's power to actualize your resolutions.

Session 5

Assignment

Read Chapters 6 and 7 before the session begins. This session will be quite different from the others since the pastor will be the focal point. The facilitator should be a member of the pastoral relations committee, if there is one, or whatever body is responsible for support of the pastor and pastoral ministry, unless an outside person is leading the group.

Bible Study

Read Nehemiah 2:17-18. What did Nehemiah see regarding Jerusalem's condition? What vision did he have for the city? How did he communicate with the people? What was their response? How does the vision of a leader get picked up by the people as a whole? How can individuals advance the process of the vision taking hold?

Discussion

Let the pastor take up to half an hour to sketch out his or her vision for the church, fleshed out as much as possible. This vision can cover the areas of worship, the life of the church community, and mission. After the pastor's presentation, the facilitator can lead a discussion regarding group response to the vision. What kind of future is the pastor envisioning? How can the church get there? What will need to be done to move ahead following the vision? What will need to be left behind? Are the people of the congregation ready to build together? Why or why not? How can the vision bearer be supported?

Prayer

Have one person read Exodus 17:8-13. When Moses grew weary, he needed the support of Aaron and Hur so that the battle could be won. Pray about how each of you can support the pastor in the work of renewal and giving birth to the vision in your church. Begin in silence, asking God to show you at least one specific thing you can do. Then, out loud, pray for your pastor and the various components of the vision which she or he shared with you.

Session 6

Assignment

Read Chapter 8 through the Epilogue before the session begins.

Group Project

Pass out large sheets of paper, crayons, or colored markers to everyone. Each person should draw a map for the church's journey over the next five years. Where will you be going? Where is the route you will take to get there? What are the landmarks, milestones, or turns you must pass along the way to reach your destination? After fifteen minutes break into small groups of four or five (or do this part together if eight or less are in the group). Share your drawings with each other.

Bible Study

Read Isaiah 43:14-21. This was God's message to the people who were in captivity and were about to be restored to their land of promise. What is the "new thing" God is doing? How will they overcome their problems and obstacles? What kind of response is necessary to take part in this prophetic promise?

Group Discussion

What is the new thing God wants to do in your church? What would God call you to do to grow in worship? What would God call you to do to grow in your life as a gathered group of Christians, as a church community? What would God call you to do to grow in your mission? Decide who will be responsible to follow up on these components on the group's vision.

Prayer

Sit in silent expectancy. Listen. After some moments of silence, one person should read Ephesians 3:20-21. Invite people to praise God for the gifts spoken of in this passage. Pray for the release of this power in your church and in you personally. Pray for the specific vision you've discerned in this session. Pray for appropriate follow-up. Rejoice before God for what God will do and is doing among you.